Microsoft® SharePoint® Foundation 2010

Level 1

Microsoft® SharePoint® Foundation 2010: Level 1

Part Number: 084696
Course Edition: 2.0

NOTICES

HELP US IMPROVE OUR COURSEWARE

Your comments are important to us. Please contact us at Element K Press LLC, 1-800-478-7788, 500 Canal View Boulevard, Rochester, NY 14623, Attention: Product Planning, or through our Web site at **http://support.elementkcourseware.com.**

Microsoft® SharePoint® Foundation 2010: Level 1

Lesson 6: Customizing Your SharePoint Environment

Lesson 7: Creating a Team Site

Lesson 8: Performing Basic Site Administration

About This Course

In almost every office around the world, people communicate and share ideas to create products and services. This information sharing often requires the use of multiple software and web applications that do not necessarily work together perfectly. In contrast, Microsoft® SharePoint® Foundation combines familiar office tools, adds the latest technology, and extends the functionality of applications and the web into a single environment to share information and collaborate with colleagues, no matter where you are or how you access the information. In this course, as a team site user, you will create and edit content in a Microsoft SharePoint Foundation team site, and then you will also create and manage your own team site.

There was a time when individuals sat at a desk and worked on an entire project from start to finish with maybe just a few phone calls or a walk over to a coworker's desk to get some information. This approach will work for a project that involves only one or two individuals who are located in the same office, but will not be efficient for projects that require the efforts of numerous people and resources located in very diverse geographical locations. Using only email, desktop applications, and instant messaging to meet the information and communication needs of large teams and projects are cumbersome and time consuming. By implementing and using Microsoft SharePoint Foundation 2010, you can eliminate these disadvantages and leverage the power and flexibility of one of the most sophisticated software tools for team collaboration available today.

 Since the class setup requirements for this course are very complex, simulations are provided for all the hands-on activities in the course. If you choose to, you can run the simulations provided to perform the activities in class or to review after class. A detailed description of the required setup is also provided for reference, and for your use if you prefer to create a live environment for the class.

Course Description

Target Student

This course is designed for individuals who will need to access information on a Microsoft SharePoint team site or for individuals who may need to create and manage a team site.

Course Prerequisites

To ensure your success, we recommend that you first:

■ Take any or all of Element K's courses in the Microsoft Office 2010 curriculum and possess power-user familiarity with at least one of the applications.

■ Experience accessing information via a web browser.

Course Objectives

In this course, you will use, create, and edit content in a team site. You will also create and perform basic management of a team site using SharePoint Foundation 2010.

You will:

● Identify basic functions of collaboration technology and Microsoft SharePoint Foundation 2010 team sites.

● Add and modify list items and work with list views.

● Add, edit, and share documents across libraries and wikis.

● Communicate and collaborate with team members.

● Work remotely with SharePoint content.

● Customize your SharePoint environment.

● Create a team site.

● Perform basic site administration.

How to Use This Book

As a Learning Guide

This book is divided into lessons and topics, covering a subject or a set of related subjects. In most cases, lessons are arranged in order of increasing proficiency.

The results-oriented topics include relevant and supporting information you need to master the content. Each topic has various types of activities designed to enable you to practice the guidelines and procedures as well as to solidify your understanding of the informational material presented in the course.

At the back of the book, you will find a glossary of the definitions of the terms and concepts used throughout the course. You will also find an index to assist in locating information within the instructional components of the book.

In the Classroom

This book is intended to enhance and support the in-class experience. Procedures and guidelines are presented in a concise fashion along with activities and discussions. Information is provided for reference and reflection in such a way as to facilitate understanding and practice.

Each lesson may also include a Lesson Lab or various types of simulated activities. You will find the files for the simulated activities along with the other course files on the enclosed CD-ROM. If your course manual did not come with a CD-ROM, please go to **http:// elementkcourseware.com** to download the files. If included, these interactive activities enable you to practice your skills in an immersive business environment, or to use hardware and software resources not available in the classroom. The course files that are available on the CD-ROM or by download may also contain sample files, support files, and additional reference materials for use both during and after the course.

As a Teaching Guide

Effective presentation of the information and skills contained in this book requires adequate preparation. As such, as an instructor, you should familiarize yourself with the content of the entire course, including its organization and approaches. You should review each of the student activities and exercises so you can facilitate them in the classroom.

Throughout the book, you may see Instructor Notes that provide suggestions, answers to problems, and supplemental information for you, the instructor. You may also see references to "Additional Instructor Notes" that contain expanded instructional information; these notes appear in a separate section at the back of the book. PowerPoint slides may be provided on the included course files, which are available on the enclosed CD-ROM or by download from http://elementkcourseware.com. The slides are also referred to in the text. If you plan to use the slides, it is recommended to display them during the corresponding content as indicated in the instructor notes in the margin.

The course files may also include assessments for the course, which can be administered diagnostically before the class, or as a review after the course is completed. These exam-type questions can be used to gauge the students' understanding and assimilation of course content.

As a Review Tool

Any method of instruction is only as effective as the time and effort you, the student, are willing to invest in it. In addition, some of the information that you learn in class may not be important to you immediately, but it may become important later. For this reason, we encourage you to spend some time reviewing the content of the course after your time in the classroom.

As a Reference

The organization and layout of this book make it an easy-to-use resource for future reference. Taking advantage of the glossary, index, and table of contents, you can use this book as a first source of definitions, background information, and summaries.

Course Icons

Icon	Description
	A **Caution Note** makes students aware of potential negative consequences of an action, setting, or decision that are not easily known.
	Display Slide provides a prompt to the instructor to display a specific slide. Display Slides are included in the Instructor Guide only.
	An **Instructor Note** is a comment to the instructor regarding delivery, classroom strategy, classroom tools, exceptions, and other special considerations. Instructor Notes are included in the Instructor Guide only.
	Notes Page indicates a page that has been left intentionally blank for students to write on.
	A **Student Note** provides additional information, guidance, or hints about a topic or task.
	A **Version Note** indicates information necessary for a specific version of software.

Course Requirements and Setup

You can find a list of hardware and software requirements to run this class as well as detailed classroom setup procedures in the course files that are available on the CD-ROM that shipped with this book. If your course manual did not come with a CD-ROM, please go to **http://www.elementk.com/courseware-file-downloads** to download the files.

1 Introducing Microsoft® SharePoint® Foundation 2010

Lesson Time: 1 hour(s)

Lesson Objectives:

In this lesson, you will identify basic functions of collaboration technology and Microsoft SharePoint Foundation 2010 team sites.

You will:

● Define the capabilities of Microsoft SharePoint Foundation 2010.

● Identify the features of a Microsoft SharePoint Foundation team site.

Introduction

In this course, you will create and edit content in a Microsoft SharePoint Foundation team site as well as create and manage your own team site. Before you can perform these tasks, you will need to understand the capabilities of collaboration software in general and Microsoft SharePoint Foundation in particular. In this lesson, you will identify basic functions of collaboration technology and Microsoft SharePoint Foundation 2010 team sites.

Most people are familiar with email or a word processing application and how to use it on the job to perform specific tasks such as sending messages or creating documents. In contrast, Microsoft SharePoint Foundation is much more than a simple application that performs one primary function. It is a unique type of technology that combines the best features of email, project planning, calendaring, and office productivity tools with the functionalities of the web so that individuals located in different geographical locations can collaborate as efficiently as those in the same office. In order for you to make the most of Microsoft SharePoint Foundation, it is crucial that you understand what SharePoint is and how you can integrate it into your environment.

TOPIC A

Describe Microsoft SharePoint Foundation 2010

Before you can begin using Microsoft SharePoint Foundation 2010, you need to understand the technology and become familiar with the overall structure of a SharePoint site. In this topic, you will describe Microsoft SharePoint Foundation 2010.

Any new technology requires a learning curve when you encounter it for the first time. Initially, cell phones and PDAs were the cutting edge of technology. The applications and features these tools provided were fascinating but confusing. However, once cell phones and PDAs became common place, the mystery was gone and they became everyday tools just like the television or the radio. Microsoft SharePoint Foundation is a new technology that, at first glance, can seem very challenging. However, with some basic information, you can demystify the concepts and start working productively in the SharePoint environment.

Collaboration Technology

Definition:

Collaboration technology is software that enables a group of individuals to achieve a common goal by facilitating information sharing and communication in one central location. Collaboration technology organizes and stores information for project teams or departments and makes the information available to team members located all over the world. Collaboration technology is generally web based and the information is accessible via company intranet or the Internet.

Example:

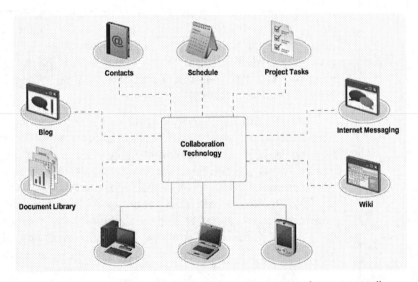

Figure 1-1: Collaboration technology enables groups to communicate centrally.

Collaboration Technology vs. Standalone Applications

Today, commonly used collaboration tools include emails, wikis, instant messaging, video conferencing, blogs, and social networking sites. Individuals use email to communicate and share documents. In contrast, a word processing program is not considered collaboration technology. Although more than one person can modify a document, a word processing application does not create a collaborative environment because it does not provide the means to share information or communicate with other individuals.

Microsoft SharePoint Foundation 2010

Microsoft SharePoint Foundation 2010 is a collaboration software product that enables individuals working on a project team or in a functional group to share information and communicate with one another from a central location. It allows users to work in a web-based collaborative environment. Microsoft SharePoint Foundation provides specialized sites that contain elements including a central calendar, task lists, libraries of documents, discussion boards and various other elements. Team members can access the site via a web browser from their PC or a PDA. SharePoint sites can be rendered offline to access information if an Internet connection is not available. SharePoint also integrates seamlessly with Microsoft Office applications in a single environment.

The Microsoft SharePoint Product Family

There are currently three products in the SharePoint family:

● Microsoft SharePoint Foundation 2010—the basic service for team site and subsite creation and administration.

● *Microsoft SharePoint Server 2010*— server application software that extends the functionality of Microsoft SharePoint Foundation 2010.

● Microsoft SharePoint Designer 2010 (SPD 2010)—web designer application software that is optimized for creating SharePoint sites.

The SharePoint Site Hierarchy

Team sites based on Microsoft SharePoint Foundation exist in a hierarchy. At the top of the hierarchy is a *top-level site* . This top-level site can have multiple subsites (including Document Workspace sites and Meeting Workspace sites), and each subsite can further contain other subsites. The entire structure of a top level site and all of its subsites is called a site collection. Permissions and navigation structure of a top-level site can be inherited by subsites, or can be specified and managed independently. In order to manage a site efficiently, the number of top-level sites has to be carefully planned.

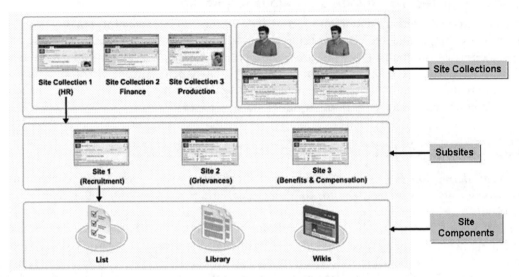

Figure 1-2: *The SharePoint site hierarchy.*

Site Collections

Definition:

A *site collection* is a virtual logical container consisting of one or more elements for grouping sites and subsites. A site collection consists of a top-level site and one or more subsites within it. The site collection has a top-level site, which enables users to navigate to the subsites present within the site. Subsites in a site collection are sets of sites that share the same owner and administration settings, security, navigation, and content structures. Users and groups can be assigned default rights at the site collection level. Users can be created at any site level and their rights modified at any subsite or item level.

Example:

For example, in any organization, there will be several departments such as human resources, administration, production, marketing, and maintenance. Each department may have several subdivisions. So, each division might have its own site collection containing various subsites. Specifically, the human resource department may have a recruitment division, benefits and compensation division, and a grievances division. Therefore, the HR department might have its own site collection and top-level site, and each HR subdivision can have individual subsites within the collection. This site and the subsites together form a logical group.

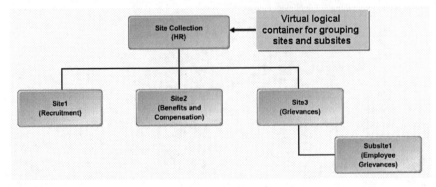

Figure 1-3: *A site collection.*

Team Sites

A *team site* is a site in SharePoint created using a default site template and is intended to facilitate team collaboration. A team site can have subsites; for instance, specific to various sub-departments of a team. It is the central location to access information and also the location to facilitate communication between team members. Each team site contains basic elements including a title, a logo, navigation tools, and content.

Figure 1-4: *A team site.*

The Top-Level or Default Site

In some instances, the team site is the default site or the top-level site. But, a top-level site does not necessarily have to be the team site.

Content Structures

The two most common categories of content structures in a Microsoft SharePoint Foundation site are lists and libraries.

Content Structure	Description
List	Stores individual items such as calendar entries, tasks, contact information, and announcements.
Library	Contains files including documents, pictures, and forms.

 SharePoint sites also store content in discussion boards, wikis, blogs, and surveys.

SharePoint Access Groups

Access to a SharePoint site is determined primarily by three groups. Each group is granted a different level of access to a site.

Group	Access Rights
Visitors	Have permissions only to view or read content.
Members	Have permissions to read, contribute, modify, and delete site content.
Owners	Have same permissions as a member with additional permissions to approve content, create new sites and content structures, and modify the overall site.

Permission Levels

Permission levels are rights granted to a user over the content on a SharePoint site. You can use the default permission levels or create a custom permission level with specific permissions that you want to assign to a group.

The following table describes the various permission levels.

Permission Level	Allows You To
Full Control	Have full control of site content.
Design	View, add, update, delete, approve, and customize content on a site.
Contribute	View, add, update, and delete content on a site.
Read	Only view content only without making any changes.
Limited Access	View specific content when given permission.
Approve	Edit and approve pages, list items, and documents.
Manage Hierarchy	Create sites, and edit pages, list items, and documents.
Restricted Read	View pages and documents, but not historical versions or user rights information.

Handwritten notes in margins:

Sales
Finance
RBMs
Co Admin
Tech

Look at current lists for guideline

Use Toplink from parent site

Webparts are shortcuts

Different Permissions for (Contract documents)

Putting people into groups and assign permissions

ACTIVITY 1-1

Understanding Collaboration Technology and Microsoft SharePoint Foundation 2010

Scenario:

In this activity, you will discuss collaborative technology and Microsoft SharePoint Foundation 2010.

1. **What are the main goals of collaboration technology?**

2. **With the rest of the class, brainstorm examples of collaboration technology. Then, discuss the resulting list of examples.**

3. **Which of these could be considered collaborative technology?**

   a) A Microsoft Excel spreadsheet with OLE links to a Microsoft Access database.

   b) A static web page that describes a company's organization.

   c) An email program such as Microsoft Outlook.

   d) A dynamic web page that enables colleagues to share information via discussion boards, blogs, and shared documents.

4. **What are the main components of a Microsoft SharePoint Foundation site?**

   a) Top-level site

   b) Sidebar

   c) Subsite

   d) Database

5. **Which of these SharePoint components is created using a default site template and is intended to facilitate team collaboration?**

   a) Subsite

   b) Team Site

   c) Corporate Website

   d) Top-level site

Pictures of everyone
Calendar of Birthdays - Reminders?

Pictures are stored
in Site Assets.
Make Title same as
descriptions.

6. True or False? The two most common categories of content structures in a SharePoint site are pictures and libraries.

___ True

___ False

10 Create a link to subsite

Editing Tools → Insert Web Part → add

Title wp

Lists - Defaults with several templates. Click on anyone and it takes you to list. webpart not separate just shortcut.

Copy URL → Site Acstions → Site Settings → Look & feel → Navigation
Edit & Sorting
Right hand side → Lists - Add link → OK → OK

Pg 138 Creates Site Shows different templates   139 Workspace

TOPIC B

Describe the Team Site Interface Elements

Now that you are familiar with the purpose of Microsoft SharePoint Foundation, the next step is to familiarize yourself with the application and interface elements and navigate around the site. In this topic, you will identify the features of Microsoft SharePoint Foundation team site.

You are an end user of Microsoft SharePoint Foundation team site. In order to access the shared information and communicate effectively with your team members you decide to familiarize yourself with the layout, the navigation tools, and the content structures of a team site.

Interface Elements

SharePoint Foundation 2010 provides an easy-to-use Graphical User Interface (GUI). There are several interface elements in Microsoft SharePoint Foundation 2010.

Interface Element	Purpose
Ribbon	Enables you to perform simple and advanced operations without having to navigate extensively. It contains the **Navigate Up** button which displays a breadcrumb trail of the pages that you have visited. Therefore, navigating through pages becomes faster and easier for anyone who is working in a SharePoint environment. When you access several pages in a SharePoint site, the breadcrumb trail helps you navigate to the parent page easily. The **Edit** button enables you to edit the current page content on a SharePoint team site. This button is most often used while customizing the SharePoint environment. It also contains the **Browse** and the **Page** tabs. In addition to these, it contains the **Site Actions** menu and the **Open Menu** drop-down menu, which is located on the extreme right corner.
The **Page Title** link	Provides a sequential list of links through navigation, from the current page shown on screen to the first page accessed in the site.
The **Top Links** bar	Shows the name of each subsite in a clickable tab across the top of the page. It contains the **Search** text box which enables you to search for content or people on your SharePoint site. The **Help** button on its extreme right corner helps you gain information about the site and the various options available in order to deploy each of them.

Interface Element	Purpose
The **Quick Launch** bar	Displays links to various lists and libraries. Apart from links to lists and libraries, the **Quick Launch** bar contains links such as **All Site Content** and **Recycle Bin**. When you click the **All Site Content** link, it displays the **All Site Content** page, which contains the lists and libraries categorized into groups. In contrast, the **Recycle Bin** enables you to restore or empty deleted items.
The Getting Started section	The **Getting Started** section contains four links: **Share this site**, **Change site theme**, **Set a site icon** and **Customize the Quick Launch.**

1. The **Share this site** link allows site owners and administrators to assign permission levels to users and groups.

2. The **Change site theme** link enables you to set the font and color scheme for your site. You can also import new themes to the theme gallery. The default themes may include **Mission**, **Vantage**, **Ricasso**, and **Yoshi**.

3. The **Set a site icon** link enables site owners and administrators to set the site title, which is displayed on each page and also the description on the home page. You can also use this option to upload images as logos for your site.

4. The **Customize the Quick Launch** link enables site owners and administrators to change links and headings on the **Quick Launch** bar.

The Ribbon

The ribbon provides several components in a SharePoint site that each enable you to perform several operations without having to navigate extensively.

Figure 1-5: *Components of the Ribbon.*

Ribbon Component	Description
The **Navigate Up** button	Displays a breadcrumb trail of pages that you visited. Therefore, navigating through pages has become faster and easier in a SharePoint environment.
The **Edit** button	Enables you to edit the current page content on a SharePoint team site. This button is most often used while customizing the SharePoint environment.
The **Site Actions** menu	Allows you to edit, format, and align the contents of a page, and create a new page, site, and site components such as lists and libraries. In addition, it allows you to manage permissions and provides you with access to all the settings of a site. Permissions and settings for a site can be configured only by a site owner.
The **Open Menu**	Enables you to navigate to your personal site, request access for a site, modify user information and settings, change the user sign in, and log out of the site.
The **Browse** tab	Enables you to navigate to the desired page in the site hierarchy.

The Quick Launch Bar

The **Quick Launch** bar provides several components that each enable you to navigate to the various pages in the site quickly.

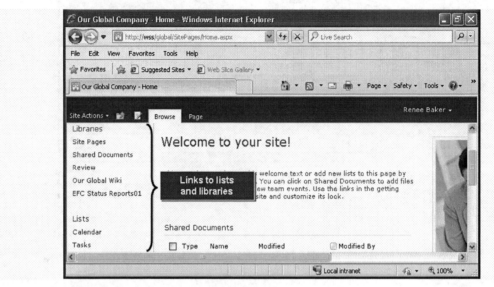

Figure 1-6: Components of the Quick Launch bar.

Component	Description
Links to lists and libraries	Displays links to various lists and libraries in the site. While creating a list or library, you can specify options that enable you to display the list or library on the **Quick Launch** bar.
The **All Site Content** link	Displays the **All Site Content** page, which contains the lists and libraries categorized as groups.
The **Recycle Bin** link	Enables you to restore or empty deleted items. The *Recycle Bin* in a SharePoint Foundation site is similar to your Windows Recycle Bin.

The Getting Started Section

The **Getting Started** section has several components that enable you to customize the appearance and navigation of the site.

Figure 1-7: *The Getting Started section.*

Component	Description
The **Share this site** link	Allows site owners and administrators to assign permission levels to users and groups.
The **Change site theme** link	Enables you to set the font and color scheme for your site. You can also import new themes to the themes gallery.
The **Set a site icon** link	Enables site owners and administrators to set the site title, which is displayed on each page, and the description, which is displayed on the home page. You can also use this option to upload images as logos for your site.
The **Customize the Quick Launch** link	Enables site owners and administrators to change links and headings on the **Quick Launch** bar.

ACTIVITY 1-2
Navigating through a Microsoft SharePoint Team Site

Setup:

Your Windows logon name is User##, where ## is a number assigned by your instructor. Your Windows password is !Pass1234 (remember, you will need to type the Windows password exactly as shown).

Scenario:

You are employed at Our Global Company (OGC), which has just implemented Microsoft SharePoint Foundation 2010. You want to familiarize yourself with the OGC SharePoint site that has been created so that you can quickly access the desired content and work efficiently.

---

1.   Access the SharePoint team site.

   a.   Choose **Start→Internet Explorer.** Your browser opens to the Team Site web page (**http://wss/default.aspx**).

---

2.   Examine the site name, **Quick Launch** bar and the **Page** tab in the OGC team site.

   a.   Examine the site name. The name of the site is displayed in the title bar of the Internet Explorer window and also below the **Internet Explorer** address bar.

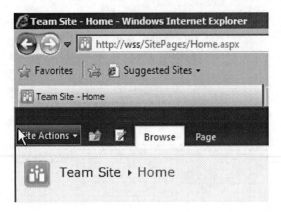

b.　Examine the **Quick Launch** bar on the left pane.

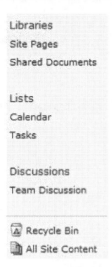

c.　Click the **Page** tab to view the ribbon interface and the various edit options available.

d.　On the ribbon, click the **Navigate Up** button.

e.　Examine the breadcrumb view of the site.

f.　On the **Quick Launch** bar, click the **Shared Documents** link.

g.　Observe that presently, there are no shared documents on this team site and the breadcrumb trail displays **Team Site → Shared Documents → All Documents.**

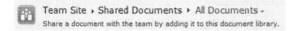

h.　On the **Quick Launch** bar, click **Calendar** to display the current month's calendar.

i.　On the **Quick Launch** bar, click **Tasks** to display the list of work that the team must complete.

j.　On the **Quick Launch** bar, click **Team Discussion** to navigate to the **Team Discussion** page.

3.　Examine the **Top Links** bar and the breadcrumb trail.

a.　On the **Top Links** bar, click **Our Global Company** to navigate to the **Our Global Company** home page.

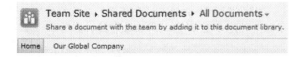

b.　Observe that the breadcrumb trail now displays **Our Global Company → Home.**

c.　On the **Quick Launch** bar, click the **Shared Documents** link.

d.　Observe that a shared document exists. On this team site, observe that the breadcrumb trail now displays **Our Global Company → Shared Documents → All Documents.**

e. On the **Quick Launch** bar, click the **Team Discussion** link. It contains a discussion topic.

f. Observe that the breadcrumb trail displays **Our Global Company** → **Team Discussion** → **Subject.**

g. From the discussion board list, click **Welcome.**

h. Observe that the welcome topic opens, and the breadcrumb trail displays **Our Global Company** → **Team Discussion** → **Welcome!** → **Flat.**

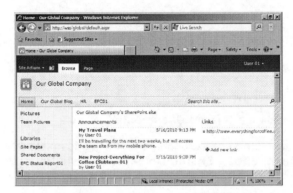

i. In the breadcrumb trail, click **Our Global Company.**

j. Observe the **Top Links** bar which displays the **Home** tab, and tabs for subsites that were created.

k. On the **Quick Launch** bar, in the **Lists** section, click **Site Links** to access the **Corporate website.**

l. Return to the team site's home page.

Lesson 1 Follow-up

In this lesson, you examined collaboration technology and Microsoft SharePoint Foundation team sites. With a solid understanding of the technology, you can begin integrating the features of SharePoint sites into your current work environment.

1. **How would using a collaboration technology like Microsoft SharePoint Foundation 2010 instead of traditional email allow your team to be more efficient?**

2. **Which navigation element would you use frequently to access content? Why?**

2 | Working with Lists

Lesson Time: 2 hour(s)

Lesson Objectives:

In this lesson, you will add and modify list items and work with list views.

You will:

● Add items to Microsoft SharePoint Foundation lists.

● Modify list items.

● Change list views.

Introduction

You have learned how to navigate within a team site and now you want to begin participating in the collaboration environment. Lists are one of the most common types of information that appears on team sites. In this lesson, you will work with lists in SharePoint Foundation.

Most of us are familiar with websites that contain unstructured information running into several pages. Trying to locate specific information from such websites only leads to frustration. On the other hand, SharePoint Foundation team sites are organized into lists that group information, which enables the easy location of needed information.

TOPIC A
Add List Items

In this lesson, you will work with lists. Before you can access list information, someone has to create it and place it at the appropriate location. In this topic, you will add items to the lists in your team site.

Almost everyone has a list or two floating around with information they use on a regular basis. The lists are written on a piece of paper, stored as a document on a computer, or saved in an email message. Each time the information changes, you have to get out the eraser or whiteout to change the hard copy, or make changes and resend an email message. Instead of going through that tedious process, you can add information to lists on a team site where the information can be updated once and available for use by everyone on the team.

SharePoint Lists

Definition:

A SharePoint *list* is a content structure that contains a group of similar items. There are different types of lists, and a team site can contain multiple lists of a similar or different type. Each site contains a set of default lists such as calendar, tasks, links, and announcements. The site owner can add other lists, if required.

Example:

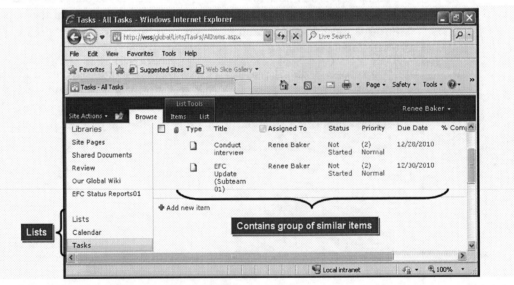

Figure 2-1: The default SharePoint lists.

Types of Lists

There are various types of lists in a SharePoint Foundation team site.

List Type	Description
Announcements	Displays short information items such as recent news or status updates.
Calendar	Keeps track of team meetings, events, and holidays in a familiar calendar view.
Links	Displays a list of links from the Internet or your company intranet.
Tasks	Stores action items for your team or a project.
Review	Enables you to track the software issues related to a type of list by assigning it to a user along with its priority level.
Contacts	Contains contact information for individuals and groups, such as clients or vendors.
Project tasks	Stores task items for a single project and provides summary info in a **Gantt** view with progress bars. A **Gantt** view is a view format type where data is displayed in a graphical format along with progress bars.
Issue tracking	Follows the progress of an issue of one or more items that are not project-related, such as support issues.
Discussion boards	Facilitates multiple discussions and newsgroups related to the organization.
Survey	Enables tracking and recording user responses to specific list of questions, thereby enabling organization to collect user preferences or data.

Datasheet view   Sequence
Standard.

How to Add List Items

Procedure Reference: Add an Item to the Announcements List

To add an item to the **Announcements** list:

1. On the **Quick Launch** bar, click the **Lists** link.
2. On the **All Site content** page, in the **Lists** section, click the **Announcements** link.
3. On the **Announcements: All Items** page, click the **Add new announcement** link.
4. In the **Announcements - New Items** dialog box, in the **Title** text box, enter the title of the announcement.
5. If necessary, in the **Body** text box, enter the body text.
6. In the **Expires** text box, click the **Date Picker** icon to select an expiration date.
7. Click **Save.**

 Generally, only the five most recent announcements are displayed on the home page. If you select an expiration date, then the announcement is displayed on the home page until that date. After the expiration date, you can access the announcement from the **All Items** view on the **Announcements** page.

Procedure Reference: Add a Calendar Entry

To add a calendar entry to a team calendar:

1. On the **Quick Launch** bar, click the **Calendar** link.
2. On the **Events** tab, in the **New** group, click **New event.**
3. On the **Calendar-New Item** page, in the **Title** text box, enter a title for the event.
4. If necessary, in the **Location** text box, type the location of the event.
5. In the **Start Time** text box, click the **Date Picker** icon to enter the start date and time.
6. In the **End Time** text box, click the **Date Picker** icon to enter the end date and time.
7. If necessary, in the **Description** text box, type a description for the event.
8. If necessary, select a **Category** for the new event.
    a. Select the **Category** option to select a type of category.
    b. Or, select the **Specify your own value** option to enter a value of your choice.
9. If necessary, check the **All Day Event** check box to make the current event an all-day event without a specific start or end time.
10. If necessary, check the **Recurrence** check box and specify the following:
    *   Select a frequency (daily, monthly, weekly, yearly).
    *   Select a pattern (once a week, bi-monthly, etc.).
    *   Select a start date.
    *   Select an end date or indicate the number of occurrences.

 Do not check the box to create a meeting workspace for the meeting unless you have been granted this permission specifically by the administrator. If you do not have permission, you can still fill out the information, but you will receive an error message that access is denied.

11. Click **Save.**

Procedure Reference: Add a Link

To add a link to a website:

1. On the **Quick Launch** bar, click the **Lists** link to display the lists.
2. On the **All Site Content** page, click the **Links** link.
3. On the **Links — All Links** page, click the **Add new link** link.

 If you want to be sure the web address you entered for a link is correct, use the **Click Here To Test** link. This will save you the trouble of opening an Internet browser and entering the link to see if it works.

4. In the **Links — New Item** dialog box, in the **URL** text box, enter the address.

 If you enter a description, this text will be used as the link instead of the web address.

5. If desired, in the **Notes** text box, enter any notes and then click **Save.**
6. If necessary, click the **Click Here To Test** link to confirm if the web address entered for a link is correct.

Procedure Reference: Add a Task

To add an item to the task list or a project task list:

1. On the **Quick Launch** bar, click the **Tasks** link or the name of the task list.
2. On the **Tasks — All Tasks** page, click the **Add new item** link.
3. In the **Tasks-New Item** dialog box, in the **Title** text box, enter a title for the task, and if necessary, click **Add** to add a predecessor to the existing task item.
4. If necessary, from the **Priority** drop-down list, select a priority level option to mention the priority for the task, and from the **Status** drop-down list, select a status level option to mention the status of task.
5. If necessary, in the **% Complete** text box, type a value that indicates the amount of work completed.
6. If necessary, in the **Assigned To** text box, enter a name to assign the task.
    *   Click the **Check Names** icon to verify if the name is typed correctly.
    *   Click the **Book** icon to browse for the name in the directory.
7. If necessary, in the **Description** text box, enter a description.
8. If necessary, in the **Start Date** text box, click the **Date Picker** icon to enter a start date, and in the **Due Date** text box, enter a due date.
9. Click **Save.**

ACTIVITY 2-1
Adding Items to SharePoint Foundation Lists

Scenario:

As a consultant with Our Global Company, you are often assigned to project teams that need to interact with client companies. Your recent assignment is to assist a company called Everything For Coffee that will implement a new HR system.

The team for this project consists of the following members:

- Bob Wheeler, Our Global Company
- Maria Calla, Our Global Company
- Chou Xen Dai, Our Global Company
- Renee Baker, Our Global Company
- Takei Soto, Our Global Company
- Lee Prentiss, Everything For Coffee
- Mattias Spindler, Everything For Coffee

You have been asked to update the Our Global Company team site to include the following information for your subteam:

- An announcement regarding the new project.
- Weekly project status meetings from 2:00 PM to 3:00 PM every Friday in the conference room.
- A link to Everything For Coffee's website (**http://www.everythingforcoffee.com**).

- A task to update the project schedule and status report before 5:00 PM every Monday.

---

1. Navigate to the Our Global Company team site, and add an announcement named *New Project—Everything For Coffee (Subteam ##)* that expires one month from today's date.

   a. On the **Top Links** bar, click the **Our Global Company** link.

       You can also click the Our Global Company link on the Quick Launch bar.

   b. On the **Quick Launch** bar, click the **Lists** link.

   c. On the **All Site Content** page, in the **Lists** section, click the **Announcements** link.

   d. On the **Announcements — All Items** page, click the **Add new announcement** link.

      ✚ Add new announcement

   e. In the **Announcements — New Item** dialog box, in the **Title** text box, type *New Project—Everything For Coffee (Subteam ##)* where ## is your user number.

   f. In the **Body** text box, type *Everything For Coffee (EFC) has contracted with us to implement a new HR system.*

   g. In the **Expires** text box, click the **Date Picker** icon, select the date that is one month from today, and click **Save** to add the new item to the announcement list.

---

2. Add calendar entries for the EFC weekly project status meetings that are to be held Fridays from 2:00 PM to 3:00 PM in your subteam's conference room.

   a. On the **Quick Launch** bar, click the **Calendar** link.

   b. On the **Calendar → Calendar** page, on the **Events** tab, in the **New** group, click **New Event.**

      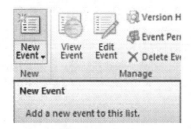

   c. In the **Calendar-New Item** dialog box, in the **Title** text box, type *EFC Subteam ## Project Status Meeting*

   d. In the **Location** text box, type *Conference Room ##*

   e. In the **Start Time** text box, click the **Date Picker** icon to select the Friday immediately following today's date.

   f. From the time drop-down list, select **2 PM** to specify the start time.

---

g.   Next to the **End Time** text box, click the **Date Picker** icon to select the Friday following the today's date.

h.   From the time drop-down list, select **3 PM** to specify the end time.

i.   In the **Description** text box, click and type *Lead consultant will provide the agenda each week.*

j.   In the **Recurrence** section, check **Make this a repeating event** to specify the recurrence.

k.   In the **Pattern** group, select **Weekly**, in the **Date Range** group, select **End after 10 occurrence(s)** and click **Save.**

Recurrence   ☑ Make this a repeating event.

3.   Add the EFC link (**http://www.everythingforcoffee.com**) to the **Our Global Company** team site.

a.   Return to the **Our Global Company** subsite.

b.   On the **Quick Launch** bar, click the **Lists** link.

c.   On the **All Site Content** page, in the **Lists** section, click **Links.**

d.   On the **Links - All Links** page, click the **Add new link** link.

e.   In the **Links - New Item** dialog box, in the **URL** section, in the **Type the Web address: (Click here to test)** text box, press the **Right Arrow** key, and type *www.everythingforcoffee.com* to enter the URL.

Type the Web address: (Click here to test)
http://www.ourglobalcompany.com

f.   If you have Internet access, click the **Click here to test** link to test if the link is working. Close the **Everythingforcoffee** browser window.

g.   In the **Type the description** text box, type a description of your choice to help differentiate between links.

h.   Click **Save.**

4.   Add a task named *EFC Update (Subteam ##)* that is of **Normal** priority, and assign the task to **Renee Baker,** with **Description** *Update project schedule and status before 5:00 PM every Monday.* Set the **Start Date** and **End Date.**

a.   Navigate to the **Our Global Company** subsite.

b.   On the **Quick Launch** bar, click the **Lists** link, and in the **All Site Content** page, in the **Lists** section, click the **Tasks** link.

c.   On the **Tasks - All Tasks** page, click the **Add new item** link.

d.   In the **Tasks - New Item** dialog box, in the **Title** text box, type *EFC Update (Subteam ##)*

e.   Beside the **Assigned To** text box, click the **Browse** button 📖 to assign the task to **Renee Baker.**

f.   In the **Select People and Groups—Webpage Dialog** dialog box, in the **Find** text box, type *baker* and click the **Search** icon.

g.   Double-click **Renee Baker** to add the user to the **Assigned To** text box.

Assigned To	Renee Baker ;

h.   In the **Description** text box, type *Update project schedule and status before 5:00 PM every Monday.*

i.   In the **Start Date** text box, click the **Date Picker** icon, and select the first Monday following today's date to specify the start date.

j.   In the **Due Date** text box, click the **Date Picker** icon, and select the Monday following today's date to specify the end date and click **Save.**

> The actual date that you select does not matter, as long as it is in the future. This applies to all dates that you select throughout this course.

5.   Add another task named *Review EFC Update (Subteam ##)* of **Normal** priority, assigned to you, with the **Description** *Review schedule and status report.* Set the **Start Date** as Tuesday following today's date and next Wednesday as the end date.

a.   On the **Tasks — All Tasks** page, click the **Add new item** link.

b.   In the **Tasks - New Item** dialog box, in the **Title** text box, type *Review EFC Update (Subteam ##)*

c.   In the **Assigned To** text box, click the **Browse** button to assign the task to **user ##**

d.   In the **Description** text box, type *Review schedule and status report.*

e.   In the **Start Date** text box, click the **Date Picker** icon, and select the first Tuesday following today's date to specify the start date.

f.   In the **Due Date** text box, click the **Date Picker** icon to select the Friday following the specified start date.

g.   Click **Save.**

TOPIC B
Modify List Items

Now that you have added content to lists, you will invariably find you need to edit the information. In this topic, you will modify list items.

A team site would quickly become useless if you are not able to make any changes to the content. Using the most current information available is crucial to the collaborative environment. Microsoft SharePoint Foundation enables you to update information and have the updated information available to team members immediately.

List Modification Options

List modification options available on a Microsoft SharePoint Foundation team site will enable you to edit list items. There are two list modification options.

List Modification Option	Description
Edit Item	Edits an item by saving, copying, pasting or canceling an item in a list.
Delete Item	Deletes an item from a list.

Edit Modification Option Tools

The Edit Item modification option consists of various tools, which enable you to edit an item based on a specific requirement.

Edit Modification Option	Description
Save	Saves any changes made to an item.
Cancel	Cancels an item if it is not required.
Paste	Pastes an item to the required location in the list.
Cut	Cuts an item from a list.
Copy	Copies an item to a list.

The List Ribbon Interface

Each list has a unique customized ribbon interface associated with it. Similar to the **Edit Item** tool, you can choose various other tools from the ribbon to customize either the items in the list or the entire list. Every tool in the ribbon has its own function associated with it, which enables customization of the different items in the list or sometimes the entire list.

How to Modify List Items

Procedure Reference: Modify a List Item

To modify a list item:

1. On the **Quick Launch** bar, click the **All Site Content** link.
2. On the **All Site Content** page, select the list in which you have to modify an item.
3. Switch to the **All <items>** view.
4. To modify an item:
   a. On the **<List name>– All items** page, select the desired item.
   b. On the **Items** tab, click **Edit Item.**
   c. On the **<List name>– <Item name>** dialog box, modify the essential details and click **Save**.

 On most items, you can also hover over the item and then click the drop-down arrow and choose **Edit Item** from the menu.

Procedure Reference: Delete a List Item

To delete an item from a list:

1. Open the list from which you need to delete an item.
2. Switch to the **All <items>** view.
3. To delete an item:
   a. On the **<List name>– All items** page, select the desired item.
   b. On the **Items** tab, click **Delete Item.**
   c. In the **Windows Internet Explorer** message box, click **OK** to confirm the deletion of the item.

ACTIVITY 2-2
Modifying List Items

Scenario:

The EFC project team recently held a meeting on the progress of the project. As a result, there are few changes to be made in the EFC site to accommodate the meeting updates. EFC Update task has been reassigned to Maria Calla which was previously assigned to Renee Baker. The location of the second meeting of the project has been changed to conference room 02. EFC subteam project status meeting has been cancelled. Also to avoid inappropriate use of the site, you would like to tell your team members that the purpose of the EFC site is to carry out EFC's e-commerce efforts.

1. Reassign the EFC Update task for your subteam to **Maria Calla.**

   a. On the **Quick Launch** bar, in the **Lists** section, click **Tasks.**

   b. On the **Tasks → All Tasks** page, click the **EFC Update (Subteam ##)** link.

   c. In the **Tasks-EFC Update (Subteam ##)** dialog box, on the **View** tab, in the **Manage** group, click **Edit Item.**

   d. In the **Assigned To** text box, triple-click to select **Renee Baker** and press **Delete.**

   e. Type *maria calla* and click the **Check Names** icon.

   f. Click **Save.**

2. For the first calendar item, change the location of the meeting and save the changes.

   a. Navigate to the **Our Global Company** team site home page.

   b. On the **Quick Launch** bar, in the **Lists** section, click the **Calendar** link.

   c. On the **Calendar** page, click the first calendar entry item.

   Title

   EFC Subteam 01 Project Status Meeting ⊞ NEW

d.   In the **Calendar - EFC Subteam ## Project Status Meeting** dialog box, on **View** tab, in the **Manage** group, click **Edit Item.**

e.   In the **Location** text box, triple-click and enter *Conference Room ##*

f.   On the **Edit** tab, in the **Commit** group, click **Save** to save the changes.

3.   Delete the **EFC Subteam ## Project Status Meeting** event from the calendar list.

a.   On the **Our Global Company** subsite, on the **Quick Launch** bar, in the **Lists** section, click the **Calendar** link.

b.   On the **Our Global Company** → **Calendar** → **Calendar** page, click the **EFC Subteam ## Project Status Meeting** event for your subteam.

c.   On the **View** tab, in the **Manage** group, click **Delete Item.**

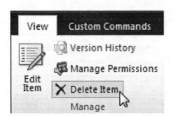

d.   Click **OK** to move the deleted item to the recycle bin.

4.   Add a note to the link for the EFC website that states, *This website is used primarily for EFC's e-commerce efforts.*

a.   On the **Quick Launch** bar, click the **All Site Content** link.

b.   On the **All Site Content** page, on the **Quick Launch** bar, click the **Lists** link. In the **Lists** section, click the **Links** list.

c.   On the **Links - All Links** page, on the **Items** tab, click the **Edit** icon next to the **EFC link.**

d.   In the **Links — EFC's website** dialog box, in the **Notes** text box, click and type *This website is used primarily for EFC's e-commerce efforts.*

e.   Click **Save.**

TOPIC C

Change List Views

In previous topics, you worked with list items in the standard list view format. If you would like to see the information displayed differently, you can select a different way to view the list. In this topic, you will change a list view.

Lists are a great way to organize information, but one long list can be a lot of information to process all at once. After you've looked at a couple of lists for a few hours, everything seems to look the same. In order to access list information more quickly, you can choose to view lists in different formats and display only the information you want.

List Views

A *list view* is a format for displaying items in a list. Each list has at least one default view that shows all the items in the list. Some lists have more than one view. Other views are available, depending on the type of list being displayed. You can change to a different view at any time without affecting the information in a list.

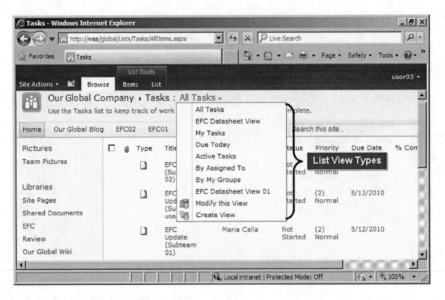

Figure 2-2: *List views for the Tasks list.*

List View Categories

There are three categories of list views available in each site.

View Category	Description
Public	A view that is visible to everyone with access to the list and appears the same to everyone who views them.
Personal	A view created by a team member and only visible to that team member. The appearance of the view is customized by the person who creates the view.

View Category	Description
Mobile	A public view that is enabled for mobile access. It formats list content to display it by meeting the requirements of the small screens of portable devices such as Personal Digital Assistants (PDAs).

View Formats

SharePoint Foundation 2010 provides you with different types of view formats.

View Format	Description
Datasheet view	Displays data in a spreadsheet format enabling quick customization and faster access.
Standard view	Displays data as seen on a web page.
Calendar view	Displays data in a calendar format by displaying the respective month, year, and week.
Gantt view	Displays data in a graphical format where tasks vary over time.
Access view	Displays forms and reports based on lists by starting Microsoft Access.

Default List Views

On a SharePoint Foundation 2010 team site, each list type has different default views associated with it.

List Type	Views
Announcements	All Items
Calendar	Calendar, All Events, and Current Events
Links	All Links
Tasks	All Tasks, Active Tasks, By Assigned To, By My Groups, Due Today, and My Tasks

 Libraries also display information in **Public, Personal**, and **Mobile** views. The default library view is the **All Documents** view.

List View Format Settings

Every list view format has a default list of options that need to be configured while creating the list view format.

Option	*Description*
Name	Displays a name for the list.
Audience	Displays the type of audience for the view format.
Columns	Indicates what columns need to be displayed on the view page.
Sort	Determines the order in which items are displayed in the column.
Filter	Indicates the items to be displayed based on certain condition.
Totals	Displays one or more totals for the column.
Folders	Specifies whether the items are viewed with folders or without folders.
Item Limit	Restricts the amount of data that the users can view in the respective view and returns the data in batches of specified size.
Inline Editing	Enables you to choose whether an edit button should be provided next to each item in the list.
Tabular View	Enables you to choose whether check boxes should be provided for each item in the list.
Style	Enables you to choose a style for the view.
Mobile	Enables you to adjust the settings for the view type.
Default Scope	Specifies the default scope for the calendar view based on the day, month, or week.

 You can find similar view options for other content structures such as libraries.

How to Change List Views

Procedure Reference: Switch a List View to Datasheet View

To switch a list view to the Datasheet view:

1. On the **Quick Launch** bar, in the **Lists** section, select the type of list.
2. On the **<List name>** page, on the **List** tab, click **Create View.**
3. On the **Create View** page, in the **Choose a view format** section, click **Datasheet View**.
4. On the **Create Datasheet View page**, in the **Name** section, in the Name text box, enter the desired name.
5. If necessary, in the **Audience** section, under **View Audience**, select the type of audience to create the view.
6. If necessary, in the **Columns** section, check all the required options that need to be displayed to select or be hidden in the **Datasheet** view.
7. If necessary, in the **Sort** section, specify the desired sort options.
   - From the **First sort by column** drop-down list, choose the default **none** option to sort the columns in which the items in the view are displayed.
   - Or, choose one or more columns based on which you want to sort the items in the list.
     1. From the **First sort by the column** drop-down list, select the desired primary column based on which you want to sort the items.
     2. From the **Then sort by the column** drop-down list, select the desired secondary column based on which you want to sort the items.
8. In the **Filters** section, choose an option to show all items or display only a subset of items in this type of view.
9. In the **Totals** section, under **Column Name,** from the necessary drop-down list, select the options that best suit your requirements.
10. In the **Folders** section, under the **Folders or Flat** option, choose an option to specify the folders through which you can navigate to view the items in the list.
11. If necessary, in the **Item Limit** section, under **Number of items to display**, choose an option to limit the amount of data that users can view.
12. Click **OK.**

 You can modify the view of a library in a similar way.

Procedure Reference: Switch a List Item View to Calendar View

To switch a list item to a Calendar view:

1. On the **Quick Launch** bar, in the **Lists** section, select the type of list.
2. On the **<List name>** page, on the **List** tab, click **Create View.**
3. On the **Create View** page, in the **Choose a view format** section, click **Calendar View.**
4. On the **Create Calendar View** page, in the **Name** section, in the **View Name** text box, enter a name.
5. If necessary, in the **Audience** section, under **View Audience**, select the type of audience to create the view.

6. In the **Time Interval** section, select the desired time interval.

    ● From the **Begin** drop-down list, choose a start time to specify the start time for those columns required to place items in the calendar.

    ● From the **End** drop-down list, choose an end time to specify the end time for those columns required to place items in the calendar.

7. In the **Calendar Columns** section, select the desired calendar columns.

    ● From the **Month View Title** drop-down list, choose an option to specify columns under the month view.

    ● From the **Week View Title** drop-down list, choose an option to specify columns under the weeks view.

    ● From the **Week View Sub Heading** drop-down list, choose an option to specify columns under the week view sub heading.

    ● From the **Day View Title** drop-down list, choose an option to specify columns under the day view.

    ● From the **Day View Sub Heading** drop-down list, choose an option to specify columns under the day view sub heading.

8. In the **Default Scope** section, from the **Default Scope** options, choose an option to specify the default scope for the view.

9. In the **Filter** section, select a type of filter to show all items in the list or a subset of lists.

10. In the **Mobile** section, select an option to adjust mobile settings for this view.

11. Click **OK.**

Procedure Reference: Switch a List Item View to Gantt View

To switch to a Gantt view:

1. On the **Quick Launch** bar, in the **Lists** section, select the type of list.

2. On the **<List name>** page, on the **List** tab, click **Create View.**

3. On the **Create View** page, on the **Choose a view format** section, click **Gantt View.**

4. On the **Create View** page, in the **Name** section, in the **View Name** text box, enter the desired name.

5. In the **Audience** section, from the **View Audience** option, select the type of audience to create the view.

6. In the **Columns** section, select the columns that you need to show or hide in the gantt view.

7. In the **Gantt columns** section, choose the desired columns that are to be presented in the Gantt chart.

    ● From the **Title** drop-down list, choose an option to specify the title for the column text field.

    ● From the **Start Date** drop-down list, select an option to specify the start date for the column list.

    ● From the **Due Date** drop-down list, select an option to specify the due date for the column.

    ● From the **Percent Complete** drop-down list, select an option to specify the percent of task completed for the column.

    ● From the **Predecessors** drop-down list, select an option to specify the predecessors for the column.

8. In the **Sort** section, specify the desired sort options.

    ● From the **First sort by column** drop-down list, choose the default **none** option to sort the columns in which the items in the view are displayed.

    ● Or, choose one or more columns based on which you want to sort the items in the list.

    1. From the **First sort by the column** drop-down list, select the desired primary column based on which you want to sort the items.

    2. From the **Then sort by the column** drop-down list, select the desired secondary column based on which you want to sort the items.

9. In the **Filter** section, select a type of filter to show all items in the list or a subset of lists.

10. In the **Group By** section, select an option to determine the way in which the items in the list will be displayed in groups and subgroups.

11. In the **Totals** section, select one or more totals to display.

12. In the **Style** section, from the **View Style** list box, choose an option to represent the style for this view.

13. In the **Folders** section, under the **Folders or Flat** option, choose an option to specify the folders through which you can navigate to view the items in the list.

14. Under **Show this view** option, choose an option to display the current view in the suitable location.

15. In the **Item Limit** section, under **Number of items to display**, choose an option to limit the amount of data that users can view.

16. Click **OK.**

Procedure Reference: Switch a List Item View to Standard View

To switch to Standard view:

1. On the **Quick Launch** bar, in the **Lists** section, select the type of list.

2. On the **<List name>** page, on the **List** tab, click **Create View.**

3. On the **Create View** page, on the **Choose a view format** page, click **Standard View.**

4. On the **Create View** page, in the **Name** section, in the **View Name** text box, enter a name.

5. In the **Audience** section, from the **View Audience** option, select the type of audience to create the view.

6. In the **Columns** section, select the columns that you need to show or hide in the standard view.

7. In the Sort section, specify the desired sort options.

    ● From the **First sort by column** drop-down list, choose the default **none** option to sort the columns in which the items in the view are displayed.

    ● Or, choose one or more columns based on which you want to sort the items in the list.

    1. From the **First sort by the column** drop-down list, select the desired primary column based on which you want to sort the items.

    2. From the **Then sort by the column** drop-down list, select the desired secondary column based on which you want to sort the items.

8. In the **Filter** section, select a type of filter to show all items in the list or a subset of lists.

9. In the **Inline Editing** section, check Allow inline editing to display an edit icon in each row so that you can edit the current row in the view without navigating to the form.

10. If necessary, choose **Tabular View** to provide individual check boxes to the items to each row.

11. In the **Group By** section, select an option to determine the way in which the items in the list will be displayed in groups and subgroups.

12. If necessary, in the **Totals** section, select one or more totals to display.

13. If necessary, in the **Style** section, from the **View Style** list box, choose an option to represent the style for this view.

14. If necessary, in the **Folders** section, under Folders or Flat, choose an option to specify the folders through which you can navigate to view the items in the list.

15. If necessary, in the **Item Limit** section, under **Number of items to display**, choose an option to limit the amount of data that users can view.

16. If necessary, in the **Mobile** section, select an option to adjust mobile settings for this view.

17. Click **OK.**

Procedure Reference: Change Calendar Settings

To change calendar settings:

1. In a SharePoint calendar, on the ribbon, on the **Calendar** tab, in the **Settings** group, click **List Settings.**

2. In the **General Settings** section, click the **Title, description and navigation** link.

3. In the **Group Calendar Options** section, under **Use this calendar to share member's schedules,** select **Yes** to create events in the calendar with attendees.

 If you want to use this calendar to scheduled resources such as conference rooms, as well as people, set **Use this calendar for resource reservation** to **Yes.** This enables you to create events in the calendar that include these resources. The **Group Work Lists** feature should be enabled by a site Owner for the **Use this calendar for resource reservation** option to appear.

4. Click **Save.**

ACTIVITY 2-3
Changing List Views

Before You Begin:

You are at the **Announcements** page of the Our Global Company team site.

Scenario:

There are various types of lists being maintained. However, you decide to organize those lists in a manner suitable to your requirement. As a part of it, you decide to change the view of the **New Project Everything For Coffee (Subteam ##)** announcement to **Calendar View** which will display respective month, week and year. You also decide to change the view of the **EFC** task to **Datasheet View** which will enable easier editing and faster customization. You decide to switch the task view from **All Tasks** to **My tasks**. Finally, you also decide to change the default **Calendar View** to **All Events.**

---

1. Change the view of the **New Project Everything For Coffee (Subteam ##)** announcement to **Calendar View** and name it **EFC Subteam Calendar View.**

   a. On the **Quick Launch** bar, click the **Lists** link.

   b. On the **All Site Content** page, click the **Announcements** link.

   c. On the **Announcements — All Items** page, in the **Title** column, check the **New Project Everything For Coffee (Subteam ##)** announcement.

   d. On the **List** tab, in the **Manage Views** group, click the **Create View** button.

   e. On the **Create View** page, in the **Choose a view format** section, click the **Calendar View** link.

   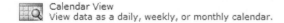

   Calendar View
   View data as a daily, weekly, or monthly calendar.

   f. On the **Create Calendar View** page, in the **Name** section, in the **View Name** text box, enter *EFC Subteam Calendar View ##*

   g. In the **Time Interval** section, from the **Begin** drop-down list, select the **Created** option.

   h. From the **End** drop-down list, select the **Modified** option.

   i. In the **Calendar Columns** section, from the **Month View Title** drop-down list, select the **Created By** option.

   Month View Title:
   Created By

j.   From the **Week View Title** drop-down list, select the **Title** option.

k.   From the **Day View Title** drop-down list, select the **Version** option.

l.   Click **OK**.

m.   Observe that the **New Project Everything For Coffee (Subteam ##)** announcement has been changed to a calendar view.

2.   Change the view of the **EFC Update (Subteam ##)** task to Datasheet view.

a.   On the **Quick Launch** bar, in the **Lists** section, click the **Tasks** link.

b.   In the **Title** column, check the **EFC Update (Subteam ##)** task.

c.   On the **List** tab, in the **Manage Views** group, click the **Create View** button.

d.   On the **Create View** page, in the **Choose a view format** section, click the **Datasheet View** link.

e.   On the **Create Datasheet View** page, in the **Name** section, in the **View Name** text box, enter *EFC Datasheet View ##*

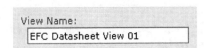

f.   Click **OK**.

g.   Observe that the announcements appear in the datasheet view.

3.   Switch the **Task** view from **All Tasks** to **My Tasks**.

a.   On the **Quick Launch** bar, in the **Lists** section, click the **Tasks** link.

b.   On the **List** tab, from the **Current View** drop-down list, select the **My Tasks** option.

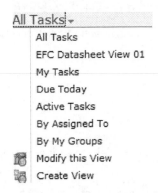

c.   Observe that only **My Tasks** tasks get displayed.

d.   Navigate to the **Our Global Company** team site home page.

4.   Change the default calendar view to **All Events**.

a.   On the **Quick Launch** bar, in the **Lists** section, click the **Calendar** link.

b.   On the breadcrumb trail, from the **Calendar** drop-down list, select the **All Events** option.

c. Observe that the calendar view gets changed to **All Events.**

d. Navigate to the **Our Global Company** team site home page.

Lesson 2 Follow-up

In this lesson, you worked with different types of lists. You added items, modified the list items, and also changed the view format of the items in the list. This will enable you to work with information in the lists in your team site. Shared information containing organized lists, enables users to efficiently locate information stored across the team site.

1. **Besides Contacts and Announcements, which lists would you and your team use the most? Why?**

2. **Which list would you modify often? Why?**

3 | **Working with Libraries**

Lesson Time: 2 hour(s)

Lesson Objectives:

In this lesson, you will add, edit, and share documents across libraries and wikis.

You will:

● Add documents to a library.

● Edit library documents.

● Share documents across libraries.

● Create wiki pages.

● Request access to a specific SharePoint resource.

Introduction

In the previous lesson, you worked with content in various types of SharePoint lists, one of the most common type of SharePoint content structures. Libraries are another common type of content structure, which enables you to collaborate with team members using larger files. In this lesson, you will work with libraries.

Lists are an ideal way of keeping track of numerous small pieces of information, but eventually you will need a place to store documents, photos, forms, and other large chunks of data. Rather than attempting to access documents from numerous locations including your computer hard drive, various network locations, and possibly hundreds of email messages, a SharePoint library provides a central location for team members to store all their necessary files.

TOPIC A
Add Documents to a Library

In this lesson, you will work with libraries. Just as you need to populate lists with content before performing other list tasks, you also need to populate libraries with the files that you need to share with the rest of your team before doing further work in the library. In this topic, you will add documents to a library.

One of the most challenging aspects of working in a team is to locate files quickly. Files are often stored in numerous locations, including the network, individual hard drives, and removable media like thumb drives. With information available in different locations, it is easy to overlook important documents or waste valuable time in creating a document that exists. In contrast, if you can both upload existing documents and create new team documents in a SharePoint library, you will have one location for every file in your SharePoint team site.

SharePoint Libraries

Definition:

A *SharePoint library* is a content structure that is used to store files. A library may contain a single type of file, such as a picture library, or it may contain multiple types of files including documents, spreadsheets, and presentations. A default SharePoint library, **Shared Documents**, is created automatically when a new team site is created. Although the **Shared Documents** library can contain multiple file types, pictures, forms, and wiki pages are generally stored in separate libraries. A site owner can create additional libraries as needed.

Example:

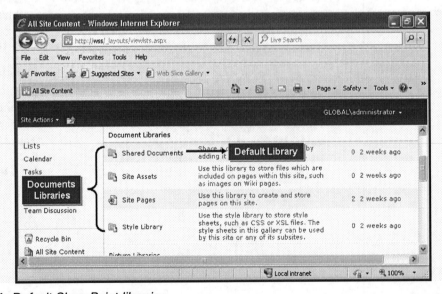

***Figure 3-1:** Default SharePoint libraries.*

Library Folders

You can create folders in most libraries. This allows you to organize files effectively in groups rather than show all files in the library as one long list.

Types of Libraries

There are four library types available in SharePoint Foundation 2010.

Library Type	Purpose
Document	Usually contains files such as documents, spreadsheets, and presentations. New files created in this library are limited to a single type of file (i.e. Word, Excel, PowerPoint) which is chosen when the library is created by the site owner. However, any type of file can be uploaded to this library.
Picture	Primarily contains pictures displayed as thumbnails. Pictures can be uploaded to the library but not created directly within the library. Specialized viewing and download options are available in addition to basic file storage.
Form	Stores XML-based (eXtensible Markup Language) forms such as invoices and expense reports used by programs such as Microsoft InfoPath.
Wiki Page	Contains linked wiki pages and supports text, pictures, tables, and hyperlinks embedded on those pages.

 Microsoft InfoPath is a program that enables efficient information gathering by providing an easy-to-do form filling in procedures that help while working with email, web browsers, or mobile devices.

Ways to Populate Libraries

Depending on how the library is configured, there are several options for placing documents into a library, including:

- Uploading from your computer, the network, or other media.

- Creating them directly in the library within the SharePoint environment.

- And, sending an email attachment to the library.

How to Add Documents to a Library

Procedure Reference: Upload Files to a Document Library

To upload files to a document library:

1. On the **Quick Launch** bar, click a document library link.

2. On the **<Library name> - All Documents** page, on the **Documents** tab, in the **New** group, choose **Upload Document** or **Upload Multiple Documents.**

   - If you chose **Upload Document:**

     a. On the **<Library name - Upload Document** dialog box, click **Browse.**

     b. In the **Choose File** dialog box, browse to the location of the file that you want to upload.

     c. Select the file.

     d. Click **Open.**

     e. If necessary, uncheck **Overwrite existing files.**

     f. Click **OK.**

   - If you chose **Upload Multiple Documents:**

     a. On the **<Library name - Upload Multiple Documents** dialog box, on the left pane, click the **Browse for files instead** link to browse the location of the file or files.

     b. On the right pane, check the files that you want to upload.

     c. Click **Open** to upload the selected files.

     d. If necessary, uncheck **Overwrite existing files.**

     e. Click **OK.**

     f. Click **Yes** to confirm the uploading of multiple files.

Procedure Reference: Upload Files to a Picture Library

To upload picture files to a picture library:

1. Click a picture library link.

2. On the **Documents** tab, in the **New** group, choose **Upload Picture** or **Upload Multiple Pictures.**

   - If you chose **Upload Picture:**

     a. In the **Select Picture** dialog box, click **Browse.**

     b. In the **Choose File** dialog box, browse to the location of the file that you want to upload.

     c. Select the file.

     d. Click **Open.**

     e. If necessary, uncheck **Overwrite existing files.**

     f. Click **OK.** The **Edit Item** page opens, where you can add or modify properties such as File Name, Title, Date Picture Taken, Description, Keywords.

At the top of the **Edit Item** page, the message "The document was uploaded successfully. Use this form to update the properties of this document." is displayed. Even if you click **Cancel** at this point, the file still appears in the picture library.

    g. Click **OK.**

● If you chose **Upload Multiple Pictures:**

    a. If necessary, in the **Microsoft Office Picture Manager** window, browse to the location of the picture files.

    b. Select the picture files that you want to upload.

    c. Click **Upload And Close.**

    d. When the **Uploading Pictures** page is displayed, click the **Go Back To <LibraryName>** link.

Procedure Reference: Create Documents in the Shared Documents Library

To create documents in the Shared Documents library:

1. On the **Quick Launch** bar, click the **Shared Documents** link.
2. On the **Shared Documents - All Documents** page, on the **Documents** tab, in the **New** group, click **New Document.**
3. To acknowledge the security message and open Microsoft Office Word 2010, click **OK.** The application opens in Compatibility Mode.
4. Enter the text and other content for the new document, and format it as necessary.
5. Click **Save.** By default, the file will be saved in the Shared Documents folder on the SharePoint server.
6. Type a file name and click **Save.**

Creating Documents in Other Libraries

Creating documents in other libraries is similar to creating documents in the **Shared Documents** library, but the specific steps depend on the configuration of the library itself. For instance, if a document library is configured so that its template is a Microsoft Excel spreadsheet, then Excel will open when you click **New Document.** However, you should be aware that there is no option for creating files in a picture library.

ACTIVITY 3-1
Uploading Documents to Libraries

Data Files:

Everything For Coffee Intro.pptx, Meeting Agendas.dotx, Everything For Coffee Project Kickoff.docx, GlobalTeamPic.jpg

Before You Begin:

You are at the **Our Global Company** team site.

Scenario:

To begin organizing the information pertaining to the EFC project, you decide to include relevant documents that currently reside on your hard drive in several SharePoint libraries. For example, you have several files on your hard drive that deal with facets of the EFC project, including:

- A PowerPoint presentation that introduced the project, Everything For Coffee Intro.pptx, which you want to place in the Shared Documents library.

- A Word template for meeting agendas, Meeting Agendas.dotx, which you also want to place in the Shared Documents library.

- The original EFC project kickoff report, Everything For Coffee Project Kickoff.docx, which you want to place in the EFC Status Reports library.

- A digital photograph of Global employees, GlobalTeamPic.jpg, which you want to place in the Team Pictures library. You also need a document on company policies for future reference so you decide to download a copy of the document.

1. Upload Everything For Coffee Intro.pptx and Meeting Agendas.dotx to the **Shared Documents** folder.

 SharePoint Foundation 2010 will not allow multiple files with the same name to reside in a library, so each person who uploads the documents will overwrite the last version of the uploaded documents.

   a. On the **Quick Launch** bar, in the **Libraries** section, click the **Shared Documents** link.

   b. On the **Documents** tab, in the **New** group, choose **Upload Document→Upload Multiple Documents.**

   c. In the **Shared Documents - Upload Multiple Documents** dialog box, click the **Browse for files instead** link.

   d. In the **Open** dialog box, if necessary navigate to C:\084696Data\Working with Libraries folder and on the right pane, select **Everything For Coffee Intro.pptx** and **Meeting Agendas.dotx** and click **Open.**

   e. In the **Shared Documents - Upload Multiple Documents** dialog box, click **OK.**

   f. Click **Done.**

2. Upload Everything For Coffee Project Kickoff.docx to the **EFC Status Reports##** library.

   a. Navigate to the **EFC Status Reports##** library.

   b. On the **Documents** tab, in the **New** group, choose **Upload Document→Upload Document.**

   c. In the **EFC Status Report## - Upload Document** dialog box, click **Browse.**

   d. In the **Choose File to Upload** dialog box, on the right pane, select **Everything For Coffee Project Kickoff.docx** and click **Open.**

   e. In the **EFC Status Report## - Upload Document** dialog box, click **OK.**

3. Upload GlobalTeamPic.jpg to the **Team Pictures** library.

a. Navigate to the **Team Pictures** library.

 Since GlobalTeam pic does not correspond to an individual user, only one student can upload the picture to the team pictures library.

b. From the **Upload** drop-down list, select **Upload Picture.**

c. In the **Team Pictures - Select Picture** dialog box, click **Browse.**

d. In the **Choose File to Upload** dialog box, select **GlobalTeamPic.jpg** and click **Open.**

e. In the **Team Pictures - Select Picture** dialog box, click **OK.**

f. In the **Team Pictures** dialog box, click **Save.**

g. From the **Actions** drop-down menu, choose **View Slide Show.**

h. Close the **Team Pictures: Slide show view - Windows Internet Explorer** window.

TOPIC B
Edit Library Documents

Now that your team has files stored in a SharePoint library, it is likely that team members will need to make changes to the files. You will need to work without overwriting each other's efforts. In this topic, you will use file versioning and check out and check in as you edit library files so that you can collaborate on content without creating conflicting versions.

If every team member could make changes to a file at the same time, the latest and the most accurate change might not be known. When members are required to check out files in order to edit them, an orderly sequence of changes is created, and each member can make sure that their changes are not lost or overwritten.

Versions

Definition:

Versions are successive copies of a document that are created each time the file is modified. A version number is assigned to each copy. The version number, a description of the modification, and the date the file was modified are all visible in the document library. Using versions allows a file to be reverted back to an earlier copy or recovered if it is accidentally deleted. Versioning is not enabled in SharePoint by default, but it can be enabled by the site owner. Versioning can be enabled on both lists and libraries.

Example:

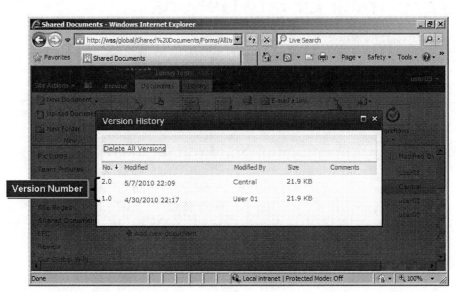

Figure 3-2: Versions of a single file in the Shared Documents Library.

Major vs. Minor Versions

Versions are classified as either major (for example, adding, changing, or deleting large sections of text) or minor (for example, updating few figures in a spreadsheet or changing the wording of a sentence). Major versions are indicated by whole numbers (1.0, 2.0, 3.0, etc.), while minor versions are indicated by decimals (1.1, 1.2, 1.3, etc.).

The Check In/Check Out Process

The Check In/Check Out process enables you to take a document out of the library, make the required changes, and put the document back into the library for other users. It prevents multiple users from editing the same file simultaneously. Each time a file is checked out, it is locked and other users can read the file but cannot edit it. The Check In/Check Out process involves a series of activities.

1. Identify the file in a library that you want to check out.

2. Once team member checks out a file, it is locked.

3. The team member makes changes and saves the file.

4. The file is checked in, and if versioning is enabled, a new version number is created.

5. And, the file is unlocked.

Editing vs. Checking Out

You can modify a file in a library either by editing it directly or by checking it out and then editing the content. If versioning is enabled on a library, each time you save a file while you are editing it directly, a version is automatically created. It does not matter how simple or complex the change is, once any change is made and the document saved, a version is assigned. In contrast, when you check out a file, you can edit and save the changes locally as many times as you want without creating new versions. A new version is not created until you check the file back in to the library.

Share and Track Library Options

There are several options to track and share a library and the changes made to it.

Library Option	Description
E-mail a Link	Enables you to send a link of a particular library to another user.
RSS Feed	Allows you to subscribe to live feeds from a library.
Alert Me	Alerts you via mail or text messages whenever changes are made to a library.

How to Edit Library Documents

Procedure Reference: Open a Read-Only Copy of a Library File

To open a read-only copy of a library file:

1. On the **Quick Launch** bar, click the desired library link to navigate to the library that holds the file you want to open.
2. Click the name of the file that you want to open.
3. In the **Open Document** dialog box, verify that **Read Only** is selected, and click **OK.**

Procedure Reference: Open a Library File for Editing

To open a library file for editing:

1. On the **Quick Launch** bar, click the desired library link to navigate to the library that holds the file you want to open.
2. Click the name of the file you want to open.
3. In the **Open Document** dialog box, click **Edit** and click **OK.**
4. When the application and file have opened, make necessary changes.
5. Save and close the file.

Procedure Reference: Check Out a File

To check out a file:

1. Navigate to the library that holds the document you need to check out.
2. Check the file that you want to check out.
3. On the Documents tab, in the **Open & Checkout** group, click **Check Out.**

 If the file to be edited is a document file with a .doc or .docx extension, then the <Application> is Microsoft Word. In a similar way, other files are opened in the applications they are associated with; for example, a .xlsx file will open in Microsoft Excel, and an Access database will open in Microsoft Access. A file cannot be edited without checking it out.

 If the file is already checked out, the Check Out option will not appear in the drop-down menu.

4. In the **Microsoft Internet Explorer** message box, check **Use my local drafts folder** and click **OK.**
5. Open **My Documents** and double-click **SharePoint Drafts** to display the checked-out file.

Procedure Reference: Cancel a File Check Out

To cancel a file check out:

1. Navigate to the library that holds the document that is checked out.
2. On the Documents tab, in the **Open & Checkout** group, click **Discard Check Out.**
3. To confirm that you want to discard the checkout, in the **Message from webpage** message box, click **OK.** All changes made to the file while it was checked out will be lost.

Procedure Reference: Check In a File

To check in a file:

1. After you have edited a checked-out document, save and close the file. You will be prompted to check the document back into SharePoint.

   - If your edits are complete, click **Yes.**
   - If you have more edits to complete, click **No.**
   - If you want to return to the document without closing it, click **Cancel.**

2. If you clicked **Yes** in the previous step, the **Check In** dialog box is displayed.

   - If necessary, enter a comment in the **Version Comments** text box.
   - If necessary, check **Keep the document checked out after checking in this version.** This option enables others to see your changes, but enables you to keep working in the file.

3. In the **Check In** dialog box, click **OK.**

4. If necessary, in the **Edit Offline** dialog box is displayed, click **OK.**

Procedure Reference: View the Version History of a File

To view the version history of a file:

1. Navigate to the library that holds the file.

2. On the Documents tab, in the **Manage** group, click **Version History.**

3. In the **Version History** dialog box, observe the date and time of modification of the document, the file size, and version comments.

4. Close the **Version History** dialog box.

ACTIVITY 3-2
Using File Check Out and Check In

Data Files:

EFC Draft Implementation Plan.docx

Scenario:

A team member wants to submit EFC Draft Implementation Plan.docx for your review. You now have to review the document and make the necessary changes. You also want to view the versioning information once you have checked in the document into the SharePoint site.

1. As the submitter, upload **EFC Draft Implementation Plan.docx** to the **Review** document library.

     A student from the first group will perform this activity.

    a. Log in to the Windows with the username *Global\User##* and password *p@ssw0rd*.

    b. Choose **Start→Internet.**

    c. In the Address bar, type **http://wss/global**and press **Enter**, to navigate to the home page of the OGC site collection.

    d. Navigate to the **Review** document library.

    e. On the **Review - All Documents** page, on the **Documents** tab, in the **New** group, click the **Upload Document** drop-down arrow and then click **Upload Document.**

    f. In the **Upload Document** dialog box, click **Browse.**

    g. In the **Choose File to Upload** dialog box, navigate to the C:\084696Data\Working with Libraries folder.

    h. In the **Choose File to Upload** dialog box, select **EFC Draft Implementation Plan** and click **Open.**

    i. In the **Upload Document** dialog box, click **OK.**

    j. Verify that the **EFC Draft Implementation Plan** document is listed in the **EFC Project** library.

2. As the reviewer, check out the EFC Draft Implementation Plan.docx file from the **Review** library.

     A student from the second group will perform this activity.

a. Navigate to the Our Global Company site.

b. Navigate to the **Review** library.

c. Place the mouse pointer over the **Type** icon and check the check box that corresponds to the **EFC Draft Implementation Plan.docx** document.

d. On the **Documents** tab, in the **Open & Check Out** group, click **Check Out.**

e. In the **Microsoft Internet Explorer** dialog box, check the **Use my local drafts folder** check box.

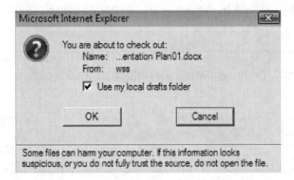

f. Click **OK** to confirm the checkout of the file.

g. Examine the icon in the **Type** column. The green downward arrow indicates the file's checked-out status.

 EFC Draft Implementation Plan01

h. Place the mouse pointer over the **Type** icon. The pop-up text displays the name of the file and the name of the user who has it checked out.

3. Revise the EFC Draft Implementation Plan.docx document and check it back into the **Review** library.

a. Open the **My Documents** folder and double-click **SharePoint Drafts.**

b. Open the **EFC Draft Implementation Plan.docx** file in Microsoft Office Word.

c. Place the mouse pointer at the end of the file, and press **Enter.**

d. Type *Reviewed and revised by Project Lead* and then type today's date.

e. Save and close the file.

f. In the **Microsoft Word** message box, click **Yes** to check the file back into SharePoint.

g. In the **Check In** dialog box, in the **Version Comments** text box, type *Project Lead review version* and click **OK.**

4. Verify whether the file has been checked into SharePoint.

a.   Observe the empty **SharePoint Drafts** folder.

b.   Close the **SharePoint Drafts** folder.

c.   Switch to **Internet Explorer** and examine the **Review** page.

d.   Refresh the **Review - All Documents** page.

e.   Observe that the **Type** icon no longer displays the checkout symbol.

---

5.   Review the versioning information for the EFC Draft Implementation Plan.docx file.

a.   Place the mouse pointer over the **Type** icon and check the check box that appears corresponding to the **EFC Draft Implementation Plan** document.

b.   On the **Documents** tab, in the **Manage** group, click the **Version History** button.

Version History

c.   In the **Version History** dialog box, observe the date and time of modification, the file size and their corresponding comments and close the dialog box.

d.   Return to the **Our Global Company** team site home page without viewing, restoring, or deleting any versions of the file.

TOPIC C
Share Documents Across Libraries

Now, you may want to share the library documents that you've been working on with specific team members. You may need to enable options that can facilitate sharing of sensitive documents across different libraries as per the business needs of your organization. In this topic, you will share documents across libraries.

An organization consists of many departments, and certain documents such as job applications might require processing from many other departments. You may need to enable the options provided in Microsoft SharePoint Foundation 2010 so that documents in a library can be shared with other libraries.

The Send To Command

The **Send To** command is used to copy a file from a library to another location. The **Send To** command also enables you to copy files between libraries and it can be accessed from a file's shortcut menu. It provides options to send the file link as email, create a document workspace, and download the file. The user should have the **Contribute** permissions for the destination library to copy files among libraries. A user with contribute permission will be able to view and update contents in a library, add contents to a library, and delete contents from a library.

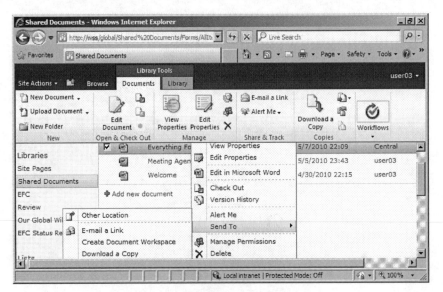

The Send To Command

Figure 3-3: *The Shared Documents library displaying the Send To command.*

 Changes made to the original library file can be updated to the copy. Similarly, any change made to the copy can also be restored to the original file.

How to Share Documents Across Libraries

Procedure Reference: Add a Send To Destination for a Document Library

To add a **Send To** destination for a document library:

 This can be configured only by the site owner.

1. Open the desired document library.
2. On the **Library** tab, in the **Settings** group, click **Library Settings** to navigate to the **Document Library Settings** page.
3. In the **General Settings** section, click **Advanced settings.**
4. On the **Advanced Settings** page, in the **Custom Send To Destination** section, in the **Destination name** text box, enter the desired library name.
5. In the **URL** text box, enter the desired URL for the document library.
6. On the **Advanced Settings** page, click **OK.**

Procedure Reference: Copy a File to a Predefined Destination

To copy a file to a predefined destination:

1. Open the desired library.
2. Open the drop-down menu of the desired file and mouse over the **Send To** option and choose the desired location.

 To be able to copy a file and share it across libraries by sending it to a predefined location, the **Send To** destination has to be enabled by the site owner. Once this option is enabled, an end user will be able to copy files to any **Send To** predefined destination.

3. If necessary, on the **Copy: <file name>** page, in the **Destination** section, modify the destination URL and rename the file.
4. If necessary, in the **Update** section, select **Yes.**
5. If necessary, in the **Update** section, check the **Create an alert for me on the source document** check box.
6. On the **Copy: <file name>** page, click **OK.**
7. In the **Copy Progress** dialog box, click **OK.**
8. In the **Copy Progress** dialog box, click **Done.**

Procedure Reference: Update Copies from a Source File

To update copies from a source file:

1. Open the library containing the source file.
2. On the Documents tab, in the **Copies group**, choose **Send To→Existing Copies** button.
3. On the **Update Copies: <file name>** page, in the **Destinations** section, check the desired check boxes.
4. In the **Copy Progress** dialog box, click **OK.**
5. In the **Copy Progress** dialog box, click **Done.**

Procedure Reference: Update Copies from the Manage Copies Page

To update copies from the **Manage Copies** page:

1. Access the desired destination library.
2. Click the desired file.
3. On the Documents tab, in the **Copies** group, click **Manage Copies.**
4. In the **Manage Copies** dialog box, click **Update Copies.**
5. In the **Update Copies** dialog box, in the **Destinations** section, check the desired check boxes.
6. In the **Copy Progress** dialog box, click **OK.**
7. In the **Copy Progress** dialog box, click **Done.**

ACTIVITY 3-3
Sharing Documents Across Libraries

Before You Begin:

1. In the **Address** bar, type *http://wss/global/hr/default.aspx* and press **Enter.**

2. Ensure that the user performing the activity has site owner permissions.

Scenario:

As a human resources department manager you have interviewed many candidates and relevant documents are uploaded to the **Interview Feedback##** document library. You want to facilitate document sharing across libraries so that the information about selected candidates can be shared with the other functional managers. You have been given site owner rights to add a

Send To destination and then share the document on selected candidates.

---

1. Add the **Shared Documents** document library as a **Send To** destination to the **Interview Feedback##** document library.

   a. On the **Quick Launch** bar, in the **Libraries** section, click the **Interview Feedback##** link.

   b. On the **Library** tab. in the **Settings** group, click **Library Settings** to navigate to the **Document Library Settings** page.

   c. On the **Document Library Settings** page, in the **General Settings** section, click the **Advanced settings** link.

   d. In the **Custom Send To Destination** section, in the **Destination name** text box, type *Shared Documents*

   e. In the **Custom Send To Destination** section, in the **URL** text box, type **http://wss/sites/global/hr/Shared%20Documents/**

   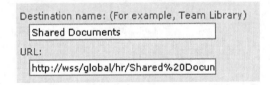

   f. Click **OK.**

---

2. Send the **List of candidates selected** item to the destination library.

   a. Access the **Interview Feedback##** document library.

   b. Verify that the **All Documents** view is selected.

   HR ▸ Interview Feedback01 ▸ All Documents ▾

c. Place the mouse pointer over the **List of candidates selected** item, and from the drop-down menu, choose **Send To→Shared Documents.**

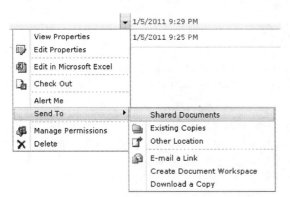

d. On the **Copy Progress** page, in the **Update** section, select the **Yes** option and click **OK.**

e. Observe the confirmation message for the copy operation and click **OK.**

f. Observe the message stating that the copy operation was successful, and click **Done.**

g. Access the **Shared Documents** document library.

h. Observe the **List of candidates selected** item being displayed.

i. Navigate to the **Our Global Company** home page.

Approach

Webpart

TOPIC D
Create Wiki Pages

In the previous topic, you shared files across libraries to centralize critical information or data. Another way to capture information from your team is to add it to a wiki. In this topic, you will create wiki pages.

SharePoint lists contain short information items, while SharePoint libraries contain entire files of information. But what do you do with information that is bigger than a list item and not quite an entire file? What about the knowledge your team members are aware of but doesn't seem to be documented anywhere? A SharePoint wiki provides a method to capture the collective information of all team members so nothing important is overlooked or lost.

Wikis

Definition:

A *wiki* is a collection of web pages that contain information created by an online community. It is a user-created knowledge base in which users add and modify content as they wish. Wikis are generally not limited to any particular subject or size. Although various levels of administration can be implemented, by default a wiki can be updated by any user who has access. A wiki can be either limited to a particular subject based on the organization's needs, or extended to include various subjects. A wiki is a dynamic content repository since it is updated continually.

Example:

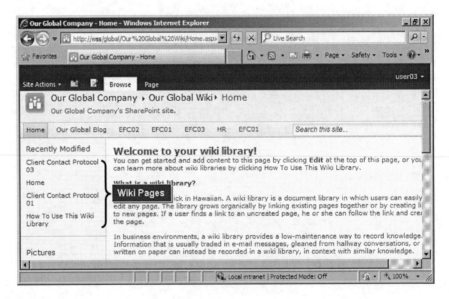

Figure 3-4: A wiki.

Wiki Technology

Wiki technology, including the Wiki markup language, is less than 20 years old. In that time, wiki-based content sites have become some of the most useful as well as the most controversial on the web, because of their open-ended, community-based approach to documentation and information sharing. You can read more about wikis and their history at one of the best-known wikis, Wikipedia, at **http://en.wikipedia.org/wiki/Wikis**.

Wiki Syntax

Wiki documents are web pages and use standard HTML web syntax, although most wikis provide a What You See Is What You Get (WYSIWYG) HTML editing tool. In addition, many wikis support some type of wiki-specific markup language or syntax, which you can use to create *wiki links* or free links between pages or between sections of a page in the wiki. Generally, these links use square bracket pairs with the target page or section name within the brackets. A wikilink to a different page looks like this: `[[page_name]]`

 HTML or Hyper Text Markup Language is the predominant markup language for creating content to display in web browsers. The HTML language contains tags with which the documents are structured.

 For information on using wiki syntax within SharePoint, click the "How To Use This Wiki Library" link on the default "Welcome To Your Wiki Library" page in a new SharePoint wiki. For more information on wiki syntax in general, see Wikipedia.

How to Create Wiki Pages

Procedure Reference: Create a Wiki Page

To create a wiki page:

1. In the **Quick Launch** bar, click the name of the wiki that you want to edit.
2. On the wiki's **Home** page, on the Ribbon, click the **Edit** button.
3. Create a link for the new page.
   a. Place the cursor where you want the link to appear.
   b. Type the name of the new page in double brackets; for example, *[[Expense Reports]]*.
   c. If necessary, enter the pipe symbol (|) and a title for the link; for example *[[Expense Reports | Submitting Expense Reports]]*.
4. On the **Format Text** tab, click **Save & Close.**
5. On the **Home** page, click the new page link.
6. In the **New Page** message box, click **Create.**
7. On the new wiki page, add the necessary content, including text, graphics, links to other pages, and so forth.
8. Format the text and other content as necessary.
9. Click the **Save** button.

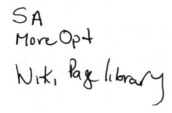

ACTIVITY 3-4
Creating a Wiki Page

Scenario:

Some of the Our Global Company members of the EFC team are relatively inexperienced when it comes to working directly with clients. You decide to create a wiki page named Client Contact Protocol that explains the importance of documenting client contact, so that this information is available to all team members. After sometime, you also notice that a wiki page you created contains a host of company guidelines that are no longer applicable and your manager has asked you to delete them.

1. Add a new section named **Contents** and a new link named **Client Contact Protocol** to the **Our Global Wiki** home page.

   a. On the **Quick Launch** bar, in the **Libraries** section, click the **Our Global Wiki** link.

   b. On the ribbon, click the **Edit** button. 📝

   c. Click at the end of the text, press the **Down Arrow** key and type **[[Client Contact Protocol ##]]**

   Hyperlinks

   Contents

   [[Client Contact Protocol 01]]

   d. Press **Enter**.

   e. On the ribbon, click the **Save & Close** button.

2. Add content to the new wiki page, format the new content, and add a link to the Home page.

   a. On the **Home** page, click the **Client Contact Protocol##** link.

   b. In the **New Page** dialog box, click **Create**.

   c. Type *Our Global Company employees should record all contact with clients. Keeping accurate records of all client interactions enables us to verify decisions that have been made and protects both the company and the individual employees in the case of any misunderstandings between Our Global Company and the client.*

   d. In the second sentence, select the word **all**.

   e. On the **Format Text** tab, in the **Font** group, click the **Underline** button.

   f. Place the mouse pointer at the end of the text and press **Enter** twice.

   g. Type *To return to the Home page, click [[Home]].*

   h. Click the **Save & Close** button.

   i. Click **Home** to test whether the new link added returns to the **Home** page.

j.   Click the **[[Client Contact Protocol ##]]** link.

k.   On the **Page** tab, in the **Manage** group, click **Delete Page** to delete the wiki page.

l.   In the **Message from webpage** message box, click **OK** to confirm the deletion of the wiki page.

Core ~~Library~~ Wiki   Alerts vs Announcements   Training Materials
   Bactec   ʼNew deals (Budgetary Quotes
   MGIT   (SMN)
   Phoenix
                                                                   ʼSample Process
   TLA   ʼCredit Process
                      {National
                      {Govt - check Platforms BAA
                      link   Sunshine

                      Change documents to be   ___
Specialty   uniform in UOM and pricing   Tools
                      case price vs bottle price   ʼPricing

   Probetec
                      Core   URLs To ^All the documents
   Viper   ~~Se~~ listPlatform   Common docs/files
   Affirm   ' Bactec (9050, 9120 [FY, FX40] MGIT
                      Phoenix (Breaker Maldi)   Capacity
   Max   TLA— (Innora, Inogula)
                                                  Create a survey

  G Cradle to grave deals
Common documents
   ʼCredit App, W-9,

   ✓Template for ToCs (Proposal templates)
   ✓Pricing Guidelines | Calculators .

   Usage Requests

TOPIC E
Request Access to SharePoint Content

In this course, you have accessed existing content on your team site. As you collaborate with individuals across your organization, you may find you need to work with lists or libraries located on other team sites or with restricted content on your team site. In this topic, you will request access to other SharePoint resources.

As a member of a team site, you generally have unrestricted access to all content on your team site. However, certain lists or libraries on your site may be restricted for security purposes, or you may need to work with content that is located on a different team site. When you are denied access to a resource, you don't have to find the correct administrator's email address, identify the resource you want access to, and compose a lengthy explanation why you need access. You can simply use the request access option on the Open menu, enter information pertaining to the access, and everything is taken care of automatically.

How to Request Access to SharePoint Content
Procedure Reference: Request Access to a SharePoint Resource

To request access to a SharePoint resource:

1. If possible, determine the URL or a detailed description of the resource you need to access so that you can include it in your access request.
2. From the **Open** drop-down menu, choose **Request Access**.
3. On the **Request Access** page, type your request.
4. Click **Send Request**.

ACTIVITY 3-5
Requesting Access to a Restricted Resource

Before You Begin:

1.

- ■ Login as **User##.**
- ■ Ensure that **User##** does not have site owner rights.
- ■

Scenario:

Your manager has gone on a vacation and delegated some of his responsibilities to you. You need to access a restricted discussion board named **Managers and Site owners** as part of your tasks.

---

1. Test your access to the **Managers and Site Owners** discussion board.

    a.   On the **Quick Launch** bar, verify that the **Manager and Site Owners** discussion board is not displayed in the **Discussions** section. Click the **All Site Content** link.

    b.   Scroll down to view the **Discussion Boards** section.

    c.   Verify that the **Managers and Site Owners** discussion board is not displayed in the **Discussion Boards** section.

---

2. Request access to the **Managers and Site Owners** discussion board from the SharePoint administrator.

    a. From the **Open Menu**, choose **Request Access**.

    b. On the **Request Access** page, type *I need to access the Managers and Site owners discussion board to fulfill my job responsibilities.*

    c. Press **Enter** and type *Thanks!*

    d. Click **Send Request.**

    e. Click the **Go back to site** link.

3. As the administrator, grant access for User## to the **Managers and Site Owners** discussion board.

    a. Open **Microsoft Office Outlook 2010** and click any of the emails requesting access to the **Managers And Site Owners** discussion board.

    b. On the preview pane, click the **Grant GLOBAL\User## access to the site** link to navigate to the **Grant Permissions** page.

    c. In the **Grant Permissions** section, from the drop-down menu under **Add users to a SharePoint group,** select **Team Site Owners (Full Control).**

    d. On the **Grant Permissions** page, click **OK.**

    e. Click the **Team Site Owners** link.

    f. Observe that **user##** who requested access for the discussion board, is displayed in the team site owners list.

4. Once the administrator has granted access, verify that you can now access the **Managers and Site Owners** discussion board.

    a. Log in as **user##** and switch to the web browser.

    b. On the **Quick Launch** bar, in the **Discussions** section, click the **All Site Content** link.

    c. On the **All Site Content** page, scroll down to view the **Discussion Boards** section.

    d. In the **Discussion Boards** section, verify that the **Managers and Site Owners** discussion board item is displayed.

    e. Click the **Managers and Site Owners** discussion board item link to view the **Welcome to the Managers and Site Owners** discussion board item.

Lesson 3 Follow-up

In this lesson, you worked with libraries. SharePoint libraries enable you to store documents, pictures, and other large files in one central location, making them accessible to everyone on your team, and enabling you to control the editing and versioning of files.

1. **What type of documents will you store in your Shared Documents library?**

2. **In your environment, what kind of wikis would you use?**

4 Communicating with Team Members

Lesson Time: 1 hour(s), 45 minutes

Lesson Objectives:

In this lesson, you will communicate and collaborate with team members.

You will:

- Participate in a discussion board.
- Contribute to blogs.
- Collaborate using the People and groups list.

Introduction

You have collaborated with team members by sharing list items and library files. But there will be instances when you will need to collaborate on ideas and concepts of team members that are not necessarily in document form yet. In this lesson, you will communicate with team members.

Numerous communication tools such as email, instant messaging, and online meetings, are available to collaborate with colleagues in a work environment. However, in order to use these tools, you have to launch several different applications. To capture the information from each application, you have to either copy and paste the information into a new file or save numerous chat conversations or emails. Microsoft SharePoint Foundation now combines all these services into a single location within your team site and captures data without significant human intervention.

TOPIC A

Participate in a Discussion Board

In this lesson, you will collaborate with other team members using various SharePoint tools. One collaboration tool that you might have already used outside the SharePoint environment is a discussion board. In this topic, you will participate in a discussion board.

In many offices around the world, email is the primary method of communicating between individuals. Email is certainly a useful tool, but in order to track conversations you end up saving multiple emails and your inbox quickly reaches capacity. Instead of carrying on a conversation by sending individual emails back and forth, you can discuss a topic, capture a conversation, and save valuable storage space by using a SharePoint discussion board.

Discussion Boards

Definition:

A *discussion board* is a method of communication that allows individuals to view and reply to messages as well as post new messages in an online forum. Message boards are generally organized into topics and each topic can contain multiple replies. Discussion boards are often moderated by an administrator who monitors message content and may also approve or reject messages before they are posted.

Example:

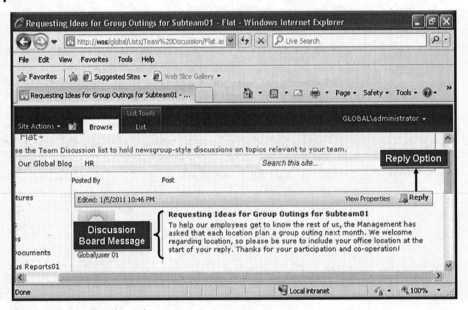

Figure 4-1: A discussion board.

Team Discussion Boards

A **Team Discussion** board is created by default when a new team site is created.

The View Properties Option

You can view the properties of the discussion by using the **View Properties** option. It displays the subject and the body text of the discussion.

Bulletin Boards and Newsgroups

Before the use of discussion boards and blogs, users shared ideas on a variety of topics via a bulletin board system. This bulletin board used dial-up connections and special software which ran over Usenet, a pre-cursor to the Internet. Bulletin boards and Usenet newsgroups were most popular from around 1980 to the mid-1990s.

Message Threads

Definition:

A *message thread* is a series of messages posted in relation to a single topic. The thread begins with an original message and contains any replies to that message. Most message threads can be sorted in chronological or reverse chronological order. A message thread allows you to follow an entire online conversation as it progresses and appears most often in email systems, discussion boards, and newsgroups.

Example:

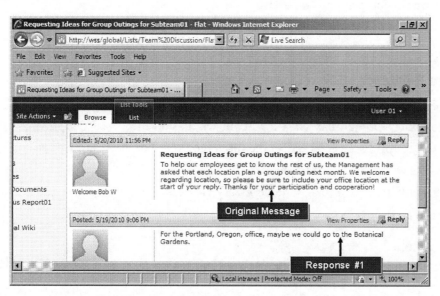

Figure 4-2: A message thread.

How to Participate in a Discussion Board

Procedure Reference: Create a Discussion

To create a discussion:

1. On the **Quick Launch** bar, click the **Team Discussion** link.
2. On the **Team Discussion - Subject** page, click the **Add new discussion** link.
3. In the Team Discussion - New Item dialog box, in the **Subject** text box, enter the subject.
4. If necessary, type the body text.
5. Click **Save.**

Procedure Reference: Add a Reply

To add a reply:

1. Click the discussion link for which you need to reply.
2. On the discussion page, click **Reply.**
3. In the **Body** text, type the reply.
4. Click **Save.**

Procedure Reference: Edit a Discussion

To edit a discussion:

1. On the **Quick Launch** bar, click the **Team Discussion** link.
2. From the list of discussions, select the discussion that you need to modify.
3. On the **Items** tab, click **Edit Item.**
4. On the **Edit Item** page, make the necessary changes.
5. Click **Save.**

Deleting an Item

You can delete an item by selecting the **Delete Item** option on the **Items** tab.

Procedure Reference: Send Alerts on a Modified Discussion

To send an alert on a modified discussion:

1. On the **Team Discussion: Subject** page, from the discussion item's drop-down menu, select **Alert Me.**
2. On the **Team Discussion: <Discussion item> - New Alert** page, in the **Alert Title** text box, enter a title.
3. In the **Delivery Method** section, select the type of delivery method for the alert.
4. In the **Change Type** section, from the **Only send me alerts when:** section, select an option to indicate the type of change that you need to be alerted to.
5. In the **Send Alerts For These Changes** section, select an option to restrict the type of alert only for a particular view.
6. In the **When to Send Alerts** section, select the desired option.
7. Click **OK.**

ACTIVITY 4-1
Participating in a Discussion Board

Before You Begin:

Log in to your user account **User ##**.

Scenario:

As a team lead, you might have to take part in various discussions regarding the upcoming activities and projects of the organization. Your manager has asked you to use the **Our Global Company's** Team Discussion page to initiate a discussion on ideas for team outing. You will update the discussions and alert the people taking part in the discussions on a weekly basis.

1. As a team lead, create a discussion topic called *Requesting Ideas for Group Outings for Subteam##* to obtain suggestion from your team members.

    a. Log in to your user account **User ##,** where ## refers to the odd student number.

    b. Navigate to the **Team Discussion** page.

    c. On the **Team Discussion - Subject** page, click the **Add new discussion** link.

    d. In the **Team Discussion - New Item** dialog box, in the **Subject** text box, type *Requesting Ideas for Group Outings for Subteam##.*

    e. In **Body** text, type *We are planning a team outing next month and would like to have suggestions regarding the location. We welcome your suggestions on it. Thanks for your participation!*

    f. Click **Save.**

2. As a member of the subteam##, reply to the discussion suggesting your favorite places. Also view the topic in **Threaded** view.

    a. Log in as user##, where ## refers to the student with even student number.

    b. On the **Team Discussion - Subject** page, click the **Requesting ideas for Group Outings for Subteam##** link that you did not create.

    c. For the **Requesting ideas for Group Outings for Subteam##** discussion item, click **Reply.**

    d. In **Team Discussion - New Item** dialog box, in the **Body** text box, type *We can go to the Botanical Gardens. It is a nice place for an outing.*

    e. Click **Save.**

    f. On the **Our Global Company → Team Discussion → Requesting Ideas for Group Outings for Subteam##** page, from the **View** drop-down menu, choose **Threaded.**

3. As the team lead of subteam##, make changes in the body text of the discussion **Requesting Ideas for Group Outings for Subteam##** and update the changes made.

    a. Log in to your user account **User ##,** where ## refers to the odd student number.

    b. Navigate to the **Team Discussion** page.

    c. Move the mouse pointer to the left of **Requesting Ideas for Group Outings for Subteam##** discussion item and check the check box that appears.

    d. On the **Items** tab, in the **Manage** group, click **Edit Item.**

e.   In the **Team Discussion - Requesting Ideas for Group Outings for Subteam##** dialog box, in the body text, click after **participation** and type *and co-operation.*

f.   Click **Save.**

---

4.   Alert the discussion board about the new updates on a weekly basis.

a.   On the **Team Discussion — Subject** page, move the mouse pointer to the left of the **Requesting Ideas for Group Outings for Subteam##** discussion item and check the check box that appears.

b.   On the **Items** tab, in the **Share & Track** group, from the **Alert Me** drop-down menu, choose the **Set alert on this item** option.

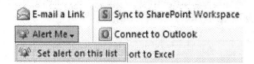

c.   In the **Team Discussion: Requesting Ideas for Group Outings for Subteam01 - New Alert** dialog box, verify the title **Team Discussion: Requesting Ideas for Subteam##** in the **Alert Title** text box.

d.   In the **Delivery Method** section, under **Send me alerts by,** verify that the **E-mail** option is selected.

e.   In the **Change Type** section, under the **Only send me alerts when,** verify that the **All Changes** option is selected.

f.   In the **Send Alerts for These Changes** section, under **Send me an alert when,** verify that the **Anything changes** option is selected.

g.   In the **When to Send Alerts** section, select the **Send a weekly summary** option.

h.   In the **Time** section, from the week drop-down list, select **Friday.**

i.   From the time drop-down list, select **10:00 PM.**

j.   Click **OK.**

TOPIC B

Contribute to Blogs

You and other team members participated in a discussion board. Blogs constitute another communication mechanism provided by SharePoint that enables individuals and teams to share ideas with a larger audience as well as to host discussions. In this topic, you will contribute to a blog.

E-mail, discussion boards, and instant messages are usually conversations between a limited number of people. You may have ideas and information that you want to share with individuals other than just team members or even outside your organization. SharePoint blogs allow you to post your ideas and provide a forum for readers to record their comments.

Blogs

Definition:

A *blog* is an online journal where a blog owner posts topics that can be read and commented on by anyone with access to the site. Blogs were originally a sort of online diary format containing individuals' personal views posted in reverse chronological order on the Internet. However, they have now evolved into important web-based sources of technical information, news, and expert opinion on a variety of topics. By default, SharePoint blogs are configured to obtain content approval from a reviewer or administrator before a post is published. They are updated on a regular basis and can be maintained by an individual or a group of users. Blog posts contain a title, content, published date and time, and a category.

A blog is short for "web log."

Example:

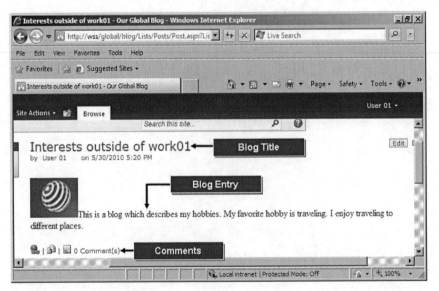

Figure 4-3: *A SharePoint blog.*

Discussion Boards Vs. Blogs

While both blogs and discussion boards can be used for team communication, each of them have a slightly different focus. A threaded discussion board is a community resource that is intended to capture posting and responses on topics that various contributors can add. Blogs in their original form were intended as a forum for blog owners, either individuals or teams, to post web content on the Internet and share views and opinions in a free-form way, without the need for sophisticated web design or editing skills. As blogs typically include areas for readers to respond to the blog topic, they can also act as discussion boards. However in standard Internet blogs, only a blog owner would post main topics.

The Links Section

The **Links** section on the home page of the team site blog contains two links, the **Photos** link and the **Add new link** link. Clicking the **Photos** link, will enable you to navigate through the various steps involved in uploading a photo to the picture library. On the other hand, the **Add new link** link will enable you to add a new link, which will provide a shortcut to the required webpage.

The Manage posts Option

The **Manage posts** option in SharePoint is a blog tool that enables you to customize the various post lists available on the blog team site. A single click of this option enables you to view the list of blogs posted by other users on the team site. Using the **Edit** button, you can modify the content present in the blog. The **Approval Status** option indicates whether the created blog has been approved or not.

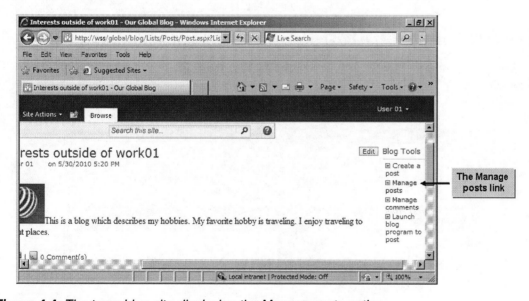

Figure 4-4: The team blog site displaying the Manage posts option.

Customizing the Posts Lists View

You can customize the view of the posts lists by changing its view. You can choose one of the options from the **All Posts** drop-down menu to change the view of the posts list.

The Manage comments Link

The **Manage comments** link enables you to make changes to the comments entered for the blog. You can customize the comments added to your blogs by choosing the **Manage comments** option available in the **Blog Tools** section.

The Archives Option

The **Archives** option in SharePoint blogs archives blog posts for future requirements. Based on the month that the blogs are created, they are archived and can be accessed later, by the blog owner or by other users. Each archived blog has a set of blog tools associated with it.

Figure 4-5: The team blog site displaying the Archives option.

How to Contribute to Blogs

Procedure Reference: Create a Blog Posting

To create a blog posting:

1. On the OGC team site, navigate to **Our Global Blog.**

2. On the **Home - Our Global Blog** page, in the right hand corner, in the **Blog Tools** section, click **Create a Post.**

3. In the **Posts New - Item** dialog box, in the **Title** text box, enter a title.

4. If necessary, in the **Body** text box, enter a body text.

5. If necessary, click **Add** to categorize the blog.

6. In the **Published** text box, click the date picker icon to enter a published date for the blog.

7. Click **Save as Draft** to save a draft copy of the blog.

 The **Approval Status** of a blog will remain pending until the site owner approves it. Only then, the blog can be published on the site. A blog can be published by a user only if the user has the site owner rights.

Procedure Reference: Add a Comment to a Blog Posting

To add a comment to a blog posting:

1. On the **Home — Our Global Blog** page, in the **Blog Tools** section, click the **Manage Posts** link.

2. From the blog lists, click the blog for which you need to add comments.

3. On the **<Blog name> — Our Global Blog** page, add the desired comment.

   1. In the **Title** text box, enter a title for your comment.

   2. In the **Body** text box, enter the text of your comment.

   3. Click **Submit Comment.**

Procedure Reference: Edit a Blog Comment

To edit a blog comment:

1. On the **Home — Our Global Blog** page, click **Manage comments.**

2. On the blog lists page, click the **Edit** button next to the blog that you need to edit.

3. On the **Comments – All Comments** page, make the necessary changes to the text based on your requirement.

4. Click **Save.**

Procedure Reference: Edit a Blog Category

To edit a blog category:

1. On the **Our Global Blog** page, on the **Quick Launch** bar, click the Categories link.

2. On the **Categories – All Categories** page, click the **Edit** button next to the category that you need to edit.

3. On the **Categories – <Category name>** page, make the necessary changes to the title.

4. Click **Save.**

ACTIVITY 4-2
Contributing to a Blog

Data Files:

Niagara.jpg

Scenario:

Your manager has informed the team that Our Global Blog has been set up for employees to use, and has asked that all team members review the blog daily. You decide to create a new blog post named "Interests outside of work" to the Our Global Blog. The blog post has to be approved by your manager. You also decide to add a interesting picture about your interests outside work to this blog post.

---

1. As an employee in a team of OGC, create a blog post named *Interests outside of work* that describes your hobbies and pets, and submit it for approval and publishing.

    a. On the **Home - Our Global Blog** page, in the **Blog Tools** section, click the **Create a Post** link.

    b. In the **Posts - New Item** dialog box, in the **Title** text box, type *Interests outside of work##*

    c. In the **Body** text box, type *This is a blog which describes my hobbies. My favorite hobby is traveling. I enjoy traveling to different places.*

    d. Next to the **Published** text box, click the **Date Picker** icon [icon] to select a publishing date in future.

    e. From the time drop-down list, select the desired time.

    f. Click **Save As Draft.**

---

2. As the manager, approve the blog created by an employee in the team.

    a. On the **Home - Our Global Blog** page, from the **Open Menu** drop-down menu, choose **Sign in as Different User.**

    b. In the **Connect to wss.ourglobalcompany.com** dialog box, in the **User name** text box, type *GLOBAL\central*

    c. In the **Password** text box, type *!Pass1234* and click **OK.**

    d. On the **Home - Our Global Blog** page, in the **Blog Tools** section, click the **Manage posts** link.

    e. Place mouse pointer to the left of the **Interests outside of work##** blog item and check the check box that appears.

    f. On the **Posts - All Posts** page, in the **Workflows** group, click **Approve/Reject.**

    g. In the **Approve/Reject** dialog box, in the **Approval Status** section, select **Approved. This item will become visible to all users** option and click **OK.**

    h. Observe that the **Approval Status** for the **Interests outside of work##** blog item has changed to **Approved.**

3. As the employee who created the blog **Interests Outside of work##**, update the blog item with pictures.

    a. Navigate to the **Our Global Blog** page.

    b. On the **Home - Our Global Blog** page, in the **Blog Tools** section, click the **Launch blog program to post** link to launch the blog program.

    c. In the **New SharePoint Blog Account** dialog box, in the **Blog URL** text box, verify if the URL is **http://wss/global/blog** and click **OK.**

    d. In the **Microsoft Word** message box, click **Yes** and **OK.**

    e. In the **Microsoft Word** application, on the **Blog Post** tab, in the **Blog** group, click **Open Existing.**

    f. In the **Open Existing Post** message box, in the **Post Title** section, select **Interests Outside of Work##** and click **OK.**

    g. In the **Microsoft Word** message box, click **Yes.**

    h. Click **Yes.**

i. On the **Insert** tab, in the **Illustrations** group, click **Picture** to upload a picture.

j. In the **Insert Picture** dialog box, navigate to the C:\084696Data\Communicating with Team Members folder, insert the **Niagara.jpg** file.

k. Click **Insert** and then in the **Microsoft Word** application, click **Save.**

l. In the **Save As** dialog box, in the **File name** text box, type **Interests Outside of Work##** and click **Save.**

m. On the **Blog Post** tab, in the **Blog** group, click **Publish.**

n. In the **Microsoft Word** message box, click **Save.**

o. Close the **Microsoft Word** application.

p. On the **Our Global Blog** page, in the **Blog Tools** section, click the **Manage posts** link.

q. On the **Posts - All Posts** page, click the **Interests outside of work##** blog item link.

r. Observe that the picture has been uploaded to the blog post.

s. Navigate to the **Our Global Company** team site.

TOPIC C

Collaborate via the People and Groups List

You communicated with other team members via discussion boards and blogs. There may be instances when you need to communicate directly with specific team members. In this topic, you will collaborate via the **People and groups** list.

When you need to communicate with team members, you could open an email application, enter the email address, assuming you know the individual's email address, and send the message. But what happens when you don't know the email address of a team member or you need to send an email to all the team members at once? Rather than hunting down email addresses and using a separate application to send your message, you can simply use the **People and groups** list on your team site to view the names of all the team members and communicate directly within the SharePoint team site.

The People and Groups List

The SharePoint **People and Groups** list contains the names of all individuals who have access to a site. By default, the list opens to the site's members group. Within this group, each team member is listed by **Name,** and additional fields display any optional information included in the member's profile. Depending upon the communication services available in the SharePoint network, team members can send email, place Internet phone calls, or send instant messages to other team members directly from this page.

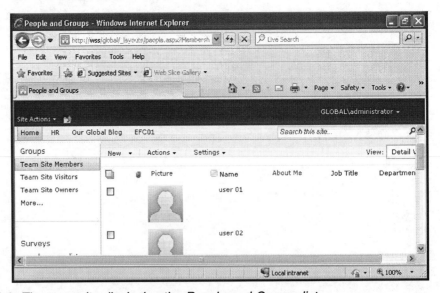

Figure 4-6: *The team site displaying the People and Groups list.*

 Other users with access to the SharePoint site and who does not appear in one of the three default groups, will still be visible on the **People and Groups** page.

The Actions Menu

You can add a hyperlink (handwritten)

The **Actions** menu on the **People and Groups** page lists various options.

 The options provided in the **People and Groups** page will enable the site owner to interact with only a specific set of users based on the requirement.

Option	Purpose
E-Mail Users	Sends email only to selected users.
Call/Message Selected Users	Calls or messages the selected user.
Remove Users from Group	Eliminates selected users from the SharePoint group.
Leave Group	Eliminates yourself from the SharePoint group.

How to Collaborate via the People and groups List

Procedure Reference: E-mail a Team Member via the People and groups List

To email a team member via the People and groups list:

1. On the ribbon, choose **Site Actions** →**Site Settings.**

2. On the **Site Settings** page, in the **Users and Permissions** section, click **People and groups.**

3. On the **People and Groups** page, select a user.

 The site owner has to add new users via the **People and groups** list for the team member to be able to collaborate.

4. From the **Actions** drop-down menu, select **E-mail Users.**

5. On the Untitled - Message (HTML) window, in the **Subject** text box, enter a subject.

6. In the **Body** text box, enter the text.

7. Click **Send.**

Procedure Reference: Add a new user via the People and groups List

To add a new user via the **People and groups** list:

1. On the Team Site home page, choose **Site Actions**→**Site Settings**.

2. On the **Site Settings** page, in the **Users and Permissions** section, click **People and groups.**

3. On the **People and Groups** page, from the **New** drop-down menu, select **Add Users.**

4. On the **Grant Permissions** page, under the **Select Users** section, in the **Users/Groups** text box, click the directory icon to search for a user to be entered.

5. In the **Send E-mail** section, observe that the **Send welcome e-mail to the new users** is selected by default.

6. In the **Subject** text box, observe the default subject that has been entered.
7. In the **Personal Message** text box, enter the text.
8. Click **OK.**

ACTIVITY 4-3
Working with the People and groups List

Before You Begin:

As an end-user, you will be performing this activity with Full Control permission over the **Our Global Company** team site. Log in as **User##.**

Scenario:

As the senior member of your team, you decide to arrange for a lunch outing tomorrow. You want to check your team members availability for lunch tomorrow, and therefore, you decide to send an email to all your team members via the **People and groups** list. You have been provided the site owner permission for the same.

1. As the senior member, send an email to your teammates from within the **People and groups** list, inviting them for lunch.

     A student from the first group will perform this step.

    a. On the **Our Global Company - Home** page, choose **Site Actions→Site Settings**.

    b. On the **Site Settings** page, in the **Users and Permissions** section, click the **Site permissions** link.

    c. On the **Permissions: Our Global Company** page, click the **Team Site Owners** link.

    d. On the **People and Groups** page, select all users present except yourself.

    e. From the **Actions** drop-down menu, select **E-Mail Users.**

    f. Observe that the **Microsoft Outlook 2010** is launched.

    g. On the **Untitled - Message (HTML)** window, in the **Subject** text box, type *Lunch tomorrow?*

    h. In the message body, type *Anyone free for lunch tomorrow? I'm available from 11:30 AM to 1:30 PM.*

    i. Click **Send.**

2. Open Microsoft Outlook 2010 and review your email messages.

     A student from the first group will perform this step.

    a. Log on to Windows as *GLOBAL\user##* with password *!Pass1234*

b. Choose **Start→Email.**

c. In the **Inbox**, click the email from **User##.**

d. Close **Microsoft Outlook 2010.**

ACTIVITY 4-4
Modifying the People and groups List

Before You Begin:

1. Launch the browser and log in as **GLOBAL\User##.**

2. Navigate to the **Team Site** home page.

Scenario:

You are a manager in OGC. A new member has joined your team. However, it becomes essential to add the new member to the **People and groups** list, thereby updating him on the latest news among the group. You want to make the group consisting of your team members as the default group in order to facilitate quicker access to the team site. You have been provided site owner permissions since you need to add new users into your team.

---

1. Add the new user **Stefan Pretsch** to the **People and groups** list.

    a. Choose **Site Actions** → **Site Settings.**

    b. In the **Users and Permissions** section, click the **People and groups** link.

    c. On the **People and Groups** page, from the **New** drop down list, select **Add Users.**

    d. In the **Grant Permissions** dialog box, in the **Select Users** section, towards the bottom-right corner of the **Users/Groups** text box, click the **Browse** icon to search for user ##.

    e. In the **Select People and Groups — Webpage Dialog** dialog box, in the **Find** text box, type *stefan* and click the **Search** icon.

    f. In the **Display Name** column, select **Stefan Pretsch,** click **Add** and click **OK.**

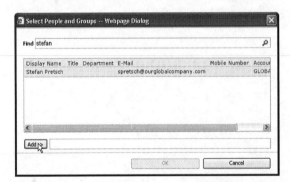

    g. In the **Grant Permissions** dialog box, click **OK** to add **Stefan Pretsch** to the **People and groups** list.

---

2. Make your team site group the default member group for the web.

---

a. On the **People and Groups** page, from the **Settings** drop-down menu, select **Make Default Group.**

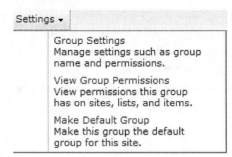

b. Observe that a message window appears prompting you to make your group the current default group for the webpage. Click **OK.**

Lesson 4 Follow-up

In this lesson, you collaborated with team members using tools such as discussion boards, blogs, and the **People and groups** list. By using the communication tools within SharePoint, you can collaborate with anyone who has access to a SharePoint site and capture feedback directly to your team site without opening other applications or files.

1. **Which will your team use more for collaboration, a discussion board or a blog? Why?**

2. **Will you and your team members use the *People and Groups* list to communicate? Why?**

5 Working Remotely with SharePoint Content

Lesson Time: 1 hour(s)

Lesson Objectives:

In this lesson, you will work remotely with SharePoint content.

You will:

● Access SharePoint content from mobile devices.

● Work with SharePoint content offline in Microsoft Office 2010 applications.

● Work offline with shared calendars.

Introduction

So far, you have worked with content in a SharePoint team site while your computer has been connected to the network. You may not always be in the office or connected to a network but you may still need access to information on the site. In this lesson, you will work remotely with SharePoint content.

Many people travel on a regular basis and do not have access to the company network. Important information can be saved on your laptop. However, you would have to transfer information to the SharePoint site once you are back in office. In some cases, you might want to work with a smaller device rather than carrying your laptop to remote locations. SharePoint provides several methods for you to access information in lists and libraries whether you carry a laptop or a PDA, and no access to the Internet is required.

TOPIC A

Access SharePoint Content from Mobile Devices

Until now, you have been accessing SharePoint lists and libraries from an office computer connected directly to a network. However, you can also connect to the network when you are not in the office and access the same sites, lists, and libraries from mobile devices. In this topic, you will view SharePoint content from a mobile device.

Most of the time, you will probably access your team site while working on your PC or laptop. However, you may be traveling to a customer site or staying in a hotel, and you prefer the convenience of working with a smaller device such as mobile devices rather than carrying your laptop. You can also connect to the network when you are not in the office and access the same sites, lists, and libraries from mobile devices. Your ability to access SharePoint content from your mobile device will help make all these aspects of your job easier.

Mobile Access

By using a Smart Phone, Pocket PC, or web-enabled cell phone, you can access SharePoint sites. A SharePoint site is displayed in a text-only format with links to lists, document libraries, and picture libraries. Once you access the home page of a site, you can navigate to the desired content by clicking text links. Through mobile access, you can work with announcements, task lists, and calendars, open and edit library files, read and author blogs and wikis, and also send emails to contacts directly from a SharePoint site. It is also possible for users to subscribe to receive alerts through text messages whenever changes are made to a particular library, list, or item. This enables users to react instantly to any critical alert generated.

 SharePoint in phones like Windows Phone 7's front end caters to the needs of Gamers and also music/film lovers.

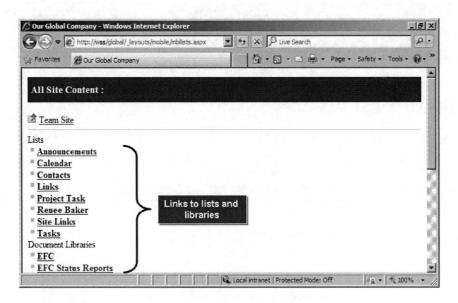

Figure 5-1: The team site displaying the mobile access links.

Mobile Access URLs

A *mobile URL* is a SharePoint web address that allows mobile devices to display SharePoint site content. Any site can be accessed from a mobile device by entering the standard URL address and replacing `default.aspx` with `m` in the address.

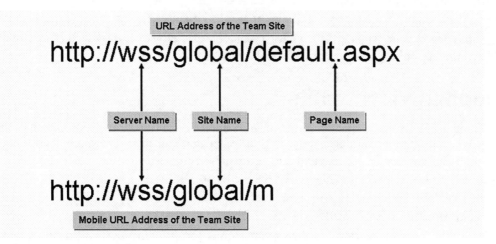

Figure 5-2: A mobile access URL.

Mobile Access to Lists

You can access a SharePoint list or library from a mobile device if you know the URL pertaining to the SharePoint list or library. However, library and especially list URLs contain coding that make the address difficult to remember. It is much easier to access the site's home page first and then click links to the list or library you want to access.

The default page, which is given to the home page of any site that is opened, is default.aspx.

Default Mobile Views

Almost every list and library has at least one default view that is enabled for mobile access.

List or Library Name	Default View(s) for Mobile Access
Announcements	All Items
Calendar	Current Events
Tasks	My Tasks, All Tasks
Contacts	All Contacts
Links	All Links
Issue Tracking	All Issues
Wiki Page Library	All Pages
Form Library	All Documents
Picture Library	All Pictures
DocumentLibrary	All Documents

Additional Mobile Views

If a list or library does not have a default view enabled for mobile access, the site owner can enable one or more standard views for mobile access. However, not all lists and libraries will have the option to enable a view for mobile access.

Mobile View Limits

Within a mobile view, specific items have character or option limits. For example, there are character limitations on the lengths of titles or of items in lists. There are also limits on the length and number of options that can be displayed in a list or in a choice field. If the text is too large to be displayed in the space available, an ellipsis (...) is displayed in place of the missing content.

Per-Item Limits for Mobile Views

The following table shows you the specific limits for different items in mobile views.

Item	Limit
Web title of a list or library	20 characters
List or library name	20 characters
List item title	20 characters
Column name	20 characters
Single-line or multiple-line text field	256 characters
Options in a choice field	10 options

Item	Limit
Choices in a choice field	10 characters
Options in a lookup list	20 options
Lookup field item	20 characters
Hyperlink or picture field	20 characters
Attachment file name	20 characters
Displayed attachments for list items	3
Calculated field	20 characters

How to Access SharePoint Content from Mobile Devices

Procedure Reference: Access the Mobile View of the Team Site

To access the mobile view of the team site:

1. On the team site home page, in the address bar, select **SitePages/Home.aspx** from the URL **http://wss/global/SitePages/Home.aspx** and type **m** to display the URL as **http:// wss/global/m**.

 The site owner has to configure mobile views for libraries.

2. Press Enter.
3. Observe the mobile view of the team site home page.

Procedure Reference: Configure Mobile Views for Libraries

To configure mobile views for libraries:

1. Navigate to the library for which you have to configure views.
2. On the **Library** tab, in the **Manage Views** group, click **Modify View.**
3. On the **Edit View** page, in the **Mobile** section, choose one of the four settings to expand the mobile page:
    *   If necessary, click **Enable this view for mobile access** to enable the view for mobile access.
    *   If necessary, click **Make this view the default view for mobile access** to set this view as the default view for mobile access.
    *   If necessary, click **Number of items to display in list view web part for this view** to set the number of items to be displayed in the list view web part.
    *   If necessary, click **Field to display in mobile list simple view** to set the field to display in the mobile list simple view.

ACTIVITY 5-1

Accessing SharePoint Content from Mobile Views

Before You Begin:

Mobile views have been enabled for the **Our Global Company** team site.

Scenario:

You and several of your team members travel extensively, but may have to work with the content stored on the **Our Global Company** team site. You decide to investigate the mobile views available before you travel.

---

1. Access the mobile version of the **Our Global Company** team site.

   a. In the browser window, log in to your user account **User##** with password as **!Pass1234** and navigate to the **Our Global Company** team site home page.

   b. In the **Address** bar of the browser, select **SitePages/Home.aspx,** type **m** and press **Enter.**

   c. Observe the mobile view for **Our Global Company** team site home page.

   Lists
   - Announcements
   - Calendar
   - Links
   - Site Links
   - Tasks

   Document Libraries
   - EFC Status Report01
   - Our Global Wiki
   - Review
   - Shared Documents
   - Site Assets
   - Site Pages

   Picture Libraries
   - Team Pictures

---

2. View the default mobile view for the **Announcements** list and add an announcement.

   a. Click the **Announcements** link.

b. On the **Announcements** page, click the first announcement link, **New Project-Everything For Coffee (Subteam 01).**

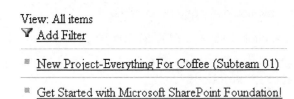

c. View the announcement and click the **Go back to list** link.

d. Click the **New Item** link.

e. On the **Announcements: New Item** page, in the **Title** text box, type your name, and then type *Travel Plans*

f. In the **Body** text box, type *I'll be traveling for the next two weeks, but will access the team site from my mobile phone.*

g. In the **Expires** text box, enter the date two weeks from today. Use the format mmddyyyy (for example, 09252010)

h. Click **Save.**

i. Click the **All Site Content** link to view the site items.

3. View the default mobile view for the **Calendar** list.

a. In the **Lists** section, click the **Calendar** link.

b. On the **Calendar** page, click the **Previous Day** link to display its corresponding calendar entry.

c.   Click the **All Site Content** link to navigate to the **All Site Content** page.

4.   View the default mobile view for the available document libraries.

   a.   In the **Documents Libraries** section, click the **EFC Status Reports##** link.

   b.   On the **EFC Status Reports##** page, in the **View: All Documents** section, click the **Everything For Coffee Project Kickoff.docx** link.

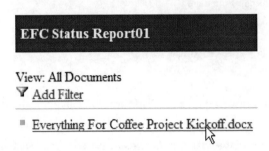

c.   In the **File Download** dialog box, click **Open.**

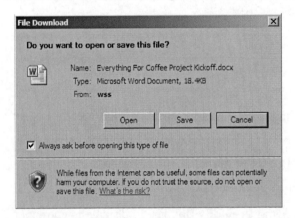

   d.   Observe the **Everything For Coffee Project Kickoff** document.

   e.   Close the **Microsoft Word** application.

   f.   Click the **All Site Content** link to navigate to the **All Site Content** page.

   g.   On the **All Site Content** page, in the **Documents Libraries** section, click the **Shared Documents** link.

Document Libraries
- EFC Status Report01
- Our Global Wiki
- Review
- Shared Documents
- Site Assets
- Site Pages

   h.   Click the **Details View** link.

i.　View the library items and at the end of the page, click **Home(Our Global Company)** link to navigate to the **Our Global Company** home page.

View: All Documents
▼ Add Filter

Name: Everything For Coffee Intro.pptx
Modified: 5/16/2010 12:12 AM
Modified By: User 01
Details

Name: Meeting Agendas.dotx
Modified: 5/16/2010 12:12 AM
Modified By: User 01
Details

Name: Welcome.docx
Modified: 5/15/2010 4:44 PM
Modified By: GLOBAL\administrator
Details

Simple View
All Site Content
Home(Our Global Company)

TOPIC B

Work Offline with SharePoint Content in Microsoft Office 2010

In the last topic, you accessed SharePoint content with a mobile device. However, if you don't have a mobile device, you can still access SharePoint content when you are out of the office. In this topic, you will work with SharePoint content offline in Microsoft Office 2010.

While traveling for business or working at a client site, you may have to access documents stored in a SharePoint library, or update list data. If you do not have access to the Internet from your location, SharePoint provides several methods of working offline with content in Microsoft Office 2010. Therefore, you can continue to view and edit data when away from office.

Offline Access

SharePoint provides offline support so that you can access SharePoint content when a network connection is unavailable (like when on an airplane or in areas with spotty network access). When you are working offline, list and library information is downloaded to your computer hard drive. You can view and edit the downloaded data using Microsoft Office (or similar) applications, depending on the type of data you want to work with. Once you are connected to the network again, some programs, such as Microsoft® Outlook®, automatically upload the changes. In other programs, such as Word 2010, you will be prompted to upload the changes.

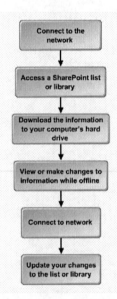

Figure 5-3: *The offline access process.*

Offline Capabilities in Microsoft Office 2010 Applications

Several applications in Microsoft Office 2010 suite are integrated with Microsoft SharePoint Foundation, so you can work offline with SharePoint libraries and lists.

Office 2010 Application	Offline Capabilities
Outlook	**Libraries**–Download a single document or an entire document library. If the library is too large, only the titles are downloaded initially. Files can be viewed in Outlook or edited in their native application.
	Lists–View and edit standard lists including: calendars, contacts, tasks, and discussion boards.
Word	**Libraries**–Use document check in and check out to edit files while working offline.
Access	**Lists**–Connect a standard or custom SharePoint list to an Access table and manage data, run queries, and create reports.

 SharePoint Workspace 2010 is a client application that offers fast, interactive access to document libraries and lists on Microsoft SharePoint Foundation 2010. It is the successor of the popular Microsoft Office Groove 2007. It also provides you with a host of automated synchronization features.

How to Work Offline with SharePoint Content in Microsoft Office 2010

Procedure Reference: Work Offline with Content in Microsoft Outlook 2010

To work offline with SharePoint content in Microsoft Outlook 2010:

1. In your web browser, open the list or library that contains the SharePoint content you need to take offline.

2. On the **<List/Library>** tab, in the **Connect & Export** group, click the **Connect to Outlook** button.

3. If necessary, in the **Microsoft Outlook** dialog box, click **Advanced,** and configure the document library or list, and then click **OK.**

4. Click **Yes** to create a folder in Microsoft Outlook 2010.
   - If you connect a library, a folder with the same name as the library is created in the **SharePoint Lists** section of the mail interface.
   - If you connect a calendar list, a folder is created in the **All Calendar Items** section of the Calendar.
   - If you connect a task list, a folder is created in the **Other Tasks** section of the **Tasks** interface.

5. Double-click the document to be changed.

6. Click **Edit Offline** and incorporate the changes you need to make.

7. Save and close the document.

8. If you are online, or the next time that you are online, in the **Edit Offline** dialog box, click **Update** to change the server copy of the document, or click **Do not update server** to leave the server copy of the document unchanged.

Procedure Reference: Work Offline with Content in Microsoft Word 2010

To work offline with content in Microsoft Word 2010:

1. In your web browser, open the list or library that contains the content you need to take offline.

2. From the document's drop-down menu, choose **Check Out.**

3. In the **Microsoft Internet Explorer** message box, check **Use my local drafts folder** and click **OK** to save the document to the **SharePoint Drafts** folder on your computer. You can now work offline with the file.

4. Use **Microsoft Word 2010** to open the document and incorporate the changes you need to make.

5. Save and close the document.

6. When you are no longer offline, check in the file so that others can view your changes.

Working with Offline Content in Other Microsoft Office 2010 Applications

Using other Microsoft Office 2010 applications such as **Microsoft PowerPoint 2010** and **Microsoft Access 2010** is similar to using **Microsoft Word 2010.**

ACTIVITY 5-2
Working with Offline Content in Microsoft Office 2010

Before You Begin:

You are logged in to your user account **User##.**

Scenario:

As you are traveling for a client meeting, you may need to work offline with some of the slides in the Everything For Coffee Intro.pptx file.

---

1. Connect the **Shared Documents** library to Microsoft Office Outlook 2010.

   a.   Navigate to the **Shared Documents** folder in the Our Global Company site in normal view.

   b.   On the **Library** tab, in the **Connect & Export** group, click the **Connect to Outlook** button.

   c.   In the **Internet Explorer** dialog box, click **Allow.**

   d.   In the **Microsoft Outlook** dialog box, click **Yes.**

---

2. Edit the Everything For Coffee Intro.pptx file to add a slide called *Next Steps.*

   a.   In Microsoft Office Outlook 2010, double-click **Everything For Coffee Intro.pptx.**

   b.   If necessary, in the **Opening File** dialog box, click **Open.**

   c.   Click **Edit Offline.**

d. In the **Edit Offline** message box, click **OK**.

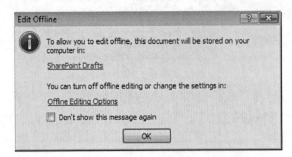

e. Select slide 5.

f. On the **Home** tab, in the **Slides** group, click **New Slide.**

g. Enter the given text in the slide.

Next Steps

- Need analysis
- Cost analysis
- Purchasing
- Installing
- Configuring
- Testing
- Training

h. Save and close the file.

i. In the **Edit Offline** dialog box, click **Update** to update the content in the server.

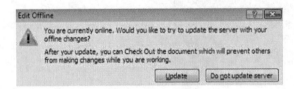

j. Close Microsoft Office Outlook 2010.

k. Refresh the browser window.

l. In the **Shared Documents** library, click **Everything For Coffee Intro.**

m. In the **Open Document** dialog box, verify that the **Read-only** option is selected and click **OK.**

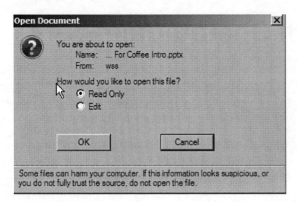

n. Select slide 6 to observe that the changes made offline are reflected.

o. Close the file.

TOPIC C
Work Offline with Shared Calendars

You used Microsoft applications, including the calendaring features in Microsoft Outlook, to access SharePoint content offline. As an organization, there may be a need to go one step further with calendaring, and enable shared calendars to facilitate collaboration and planning among the team. In this topic, you will facilitate collaboration and planning among the team.

There may be times when team members are traveling to a client's place and need to work on calendar list data with no network connection to your server. You can set various options that will enable a team member to work offline with calendar list data. Team members working offline using shared calendars will be able to increase their productivity and meet deadlines.

Shared Calendars

Shared calendars enable users to share information throughout an organization about events in a calendar. Outlook users can share their calendar events with other users and update the shared calendars in a Microsoft SharePoint Foundation team site. An event assigned to a user will automatically appear on the user's calendar. One can view multiple calendars simultaneously to schedule events, thereby preventing conflicts between events.

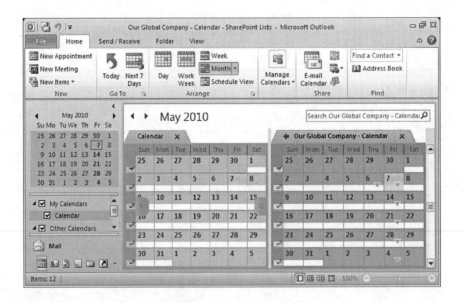

Figure 5-4: *A shared calendars view.*

How to Work Offline with Shared Calendars

Procedure Reference: Access a SharePoint Calendar Offline and Enable Sharing

To access a SharePoint calendar offline and enable sharing:

1. Access the calendar list in Microsoft SharePoint Foundation.

2. On the **Library** tab, in the **Connect and Export** group, click the **Connect to Outlook** button.

3. If necessary, in the **Microsoft Office Outlook** message box, click **Yes.**

4. In the **Other Calendars** section, right-click the calendar and choose **Open in New Window.**

5. On the **<Site name> - Calendar** window, on the **Home** tab, in the **Share** group, click **E-Mail Calendar.**

6. In the **Send a Calendar via E-Mail** dialog box, click **OK.**

7. On the **<Site name> - Calendar Calendar — Message (HTML)** window, in the **To** text box, enter the email ids of users with whom you would like to share the calendar.

8. If necessary, in the **Cc** text box, enter the email ids of users to whom you would like to send a cc of the email.

9. If necessary, in the **Subject** text box, specify the desired subject.

10. In the **Body** text box, enter the desired message.

11. Click **Send.**

Procedure Reference: Add SharePoint Calendar Events from Outlook

To add SharePoint calendar events from Outlook:

1. In the **Outlook** application, access the desired SharePoint calendar.

2. On the **Home** tab, in the **New** group, click **New Appointment.**

3. On the **Untitled - Appointment** window, enter the desired information about the event.

    1. In the **Subject** text box, type the desired subject.

    2. In the **Location** text box, type the location of the event.

    3. If necessary, check **All day event.**

4. On the **Event** tab, in the **Actions** group, click **Save & Close.**

ACTIVITY 5-3
Working with Shared Calendars

Scenario:

The HR team manager is planning an event for discussing some proposals. He would like to access and share his calendar with his teammates. The HR team manager is given access to the calendar on the **corcom** site collection in Outlook, which will enable him to share the events with others.

1. Connect the **Our Global Company** site calendar to **Outlook.**

   a. Navigate to the **Our Global Company** home page.

   b. On the **Quick Launch** bar of the **Our Global Company** home page, in the **Lists** section, click the **Calendar** link.

   c. On the **Calendar** tab, in the **Connect & Export** group, click **Connect to Outlook.**

   d. In the **Internet Explorer** dialog box, click **Allow** to open Outlook.

   e. In the **Microsoft Outlook** message box, click **Yes.**

   f. In the **Other Calendars** section, right-click the **Our Global Company - Calendar** calendar and choose **Open in New Window.**

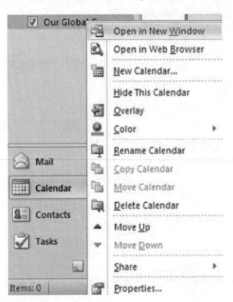

g. Resize the **Navigation Pane** to view the **Our Global Company - Calendar.**

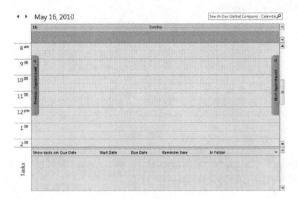

---

2. Add an event to the calendar.

   a. On the **Home** tab, in the **New** group, click **New Appointment.**

   b. On the **Untitled - Appointment** window, in the **Subject** text box, type *Newsletter Budget Proposals*

   c. In the **Location** text box, type *Conference Hall ##*

   d. Check the **All day event** check box.

   e. On the **Event** tab, in the **Actions** group, click **Save & Close.**

   f. Observe the reminder for the new calendar event and click **Dismiss.**

   g. In the **Microsoft Outlook** message box, click **Yes.**

---

3. Share the calendar with **Central.**

---

a. On the **Home** tab, in the **Share** group, click **E-Mail Calendar** and verify that **Our Global Company - Calendar** is chosen.

b. In the **Send a Calendar via E-mail** dialog box, click **OK.**

c. On the **Our Global Company - Calendar Calendar — Message (HTML)** window, in the **To** text box, type *mcalla@ourglobalcompany.com*

d. Click **Send.**

4. View the calendar events in Microsoft SharePoint Foundation.

a. Switch to the **Internet Explorer** window and refresh the page.

b. Observe that the **Newsletter Budget Proposals** event is displayed on the calendar.

c. Navigate to **Our Global Company** home page.

Lesson 5 Follow-up

In this lesson, you worked remotely with SharePoint content. Being able to view SharePoint content from mobile devices such as phones and PDAs and to edit documents and list items in compatible applications such as Microsoft Office 2010 will enable you to continue contributing to your team site even if you are traveling or working from another location.

1. **How will mobile or offline access help your team collaborate when they are not in the office?**

2. **Which application will be your primary offline editing tool? Why?**

6 | Customizing Your SharePoint Environment

Lesson Time: 50 minutes

Lesson Objectives:

In this lesson, you will customize your SharePoint environment.

You will:

● Customize personal and regional settings.

● Personalize the page view with Web Parts.

● Create an alert.

● Subscribe to an RSS feed.

Introduction

You have worked with all the components of a SharePoint site. But, as you work with SharePoint on a regular basis, you will want to customize more than just list or library views. In this lesson, you will customize your SharePoint environment.

Most of us like to customize our day-to-day activities according to our desires. We change the ring tone on our cell phone, decorate and arrange our office space, and choose our favorite home page for Internet access. All these customizations help us to use the tools more efficiently. SharePoint provides several features that you can customize to suit your environment for efficient navigation and increased productivity.

TOPIC A
Customize Personal and Regional Settings

Throughout this course, you have worked in a team site that displays generic information based on default settings. The first element of your SharePoint environment you may want to customize is your name, location, and other information that uniquely identifies you. In this topic, you will customize personal and regional settings.

In SharePoint environment, your user name is displayed on the home page and listed on the **People and Groups** page. Everyone with access to the site will only see the user name your administrator has assigned to you, and most user names are pretty generic. It is not easy to determine who "jsmith" or "mrivera" might be, and if there are two similar names, it is even more confusing. When you add personal information that identifies you and your location, everyone on the team can be sure they are collaborating with the right person.

The Open Menu

The **Open Menu** allows you to customize various aspects of the SharePoint environment.

Menu Option	Description
My Settings	Includes options to edit your personal information, change regional settings, and configure alerts.
Sign in as Different User	Displays the log on dialog box which will enable you to log on to the same SharePoint site with a different user account.
Sign Out	Signs you out of a SharePoint site completely for occasions when you are accessing a SharePoint site from a public computer.
Personalize this Page	Provides controls for you to customize your view of a SharePoint site.

My Settings

The **My Settings** menu has options to customize your personal and regional information.

Menu Option	Purpose
Edit Item	Edits personal information including your name, email address, department, job title, and also adds a picture or description of yourself.
Regional Settings	Changes the location, time zone, type of calendar, and work week.

How to Customize Personal and Regional Settings

Procedure Reference: Customize Personal Settings

To customize personal settings:

1. From the **Open** drop-down menu, choose **My Settings.**
2. On the **Personal Settings** page, click the **Edit Item** link.
3. Revise the fields as needed to include the desired information.
4. Click **Save.**

Procedure Reference: Customize Regional Settings

To customize regional settings:

1. From the **Open** drop-down menu, choose **My Settings.**
2. On the **Personal Settings** page, click the **My Regional Settings** link.
3. On the **Regional Settings** page, uncheck the **Always follow web settings** check box.
4. Make any changes necessary in the remaining sections.
5. Click **OK.**

ACTIVITY 6-1
Customizing Personal and Regional Settings

Before You Begin

1. Log in to Our Global Company site as **GLOBAL\User##.**

Scenario:

Your manager has asked all team members to include their department names and job titles in SharePoint. While adding in the details, you also decided to modify the way your name is displayed. In addition, to facilitate working with those teammates who are based overseas, you have adjusted your work schedule to begin at 10:00 AM each morning and you want to display time in a 24-hour format.

---

1. Customize your personal settings to include your name, department name, and job title.

    a. On the top-right corner of the browser window, click the down arrow next to **User##.**

    b. Choose the **My Settings** option.

    c. On the **Personal Settings** page, click the **Edit Item** link.

    d. In the **Edit Personal Settings** dialog box, in the **Name** text box, type *OGC\User##*

    e. In the **Department** text box, click and type *Client Services*

    f. In the **Job Title** text box, click and type *Senior Consultant*

    g. In the **Edit Personal Settings** dialog box, click **Save.**

    h. Observe that **OGC\User##** is displayed in the **Open Menu** menu.

---

2. Customize your regional settings to change your work week to be from 10:00 AM to 7:00 PM, Monday through Friday, and to display a 24-hour time format.

    a. On the **Personal Settings** page, click the **My Regional Settings** link.

    b. On the **Regional Settings** page, in the **Follow Web Settings** section, uncheck the **Always follow web settings** check box.

    c. In the **Define Your Work Week** section of the page, set the **Start time** to **10:00 AM** and **End time** to **7:00 PM.**

    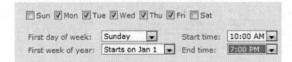

---

d. In the **Time Format** section, from the **Time format** drop-down list, select **24 Hour** and click **OK.**

Time format:

TOPIC B

Personalize the Page View with Web Parts

You customized personal and regional settings of your SharePoint team site. Further, for better interaction with your team site, you might want to personalize its different content structures. In this topic, you will personalize the page view using web parts.

Every team site has content organized in a structured format. The appearance of the team site remains the same to every member who visits the site. As long as you do not have to visit the site often, its appearance does not matter. However, there could be other sites that you have to visit more often. You might want to customize such sites in order to obtain information easily without much navigation within the site. SharePoint provides you with tools that will enable you to customize or personalize any page so that you can quickly and easily locate information within a team site.

Don't
need
Webparts
if quick
links are being
Used.

Web Parts

Definition:

A *Web Part* is the basic design element of a SharePoint site. All content on a page, whether a list, an image, or a library, is contained within a Web Part. Each page has default Web Parts that correspond to the default lists and libraries on that page. Web Parts can be moved, added, deleted, and edited directly in the browser window.

 All Web Parts are located in a gallery, similar to galleries in Word or Excel. Each site has a gallery of Web Parts.

Example:

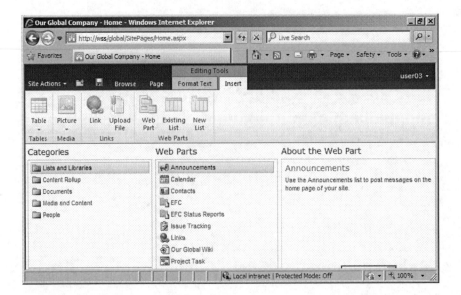

Figure 6-1: The Web Parts page

Page Views

A *page view* is a format for displaying content on a page. Each page in a site has one standard view that is visible to anyone with access to the page. This is called the *shared view*. Each member can create their own view, called a *personal view*. A personal view is only visible to the member who created the view.

 Site Visitors cannot create personal views.

How to Personalize the Page View with Web Parts

Procedure Reference: Create a Personalized Page View

To create a personalized page view:

1. Navigate to the page that you want to personalize.
2. From the **Open Menu**, choose **Personalize this Page.**
3. If necessary, add web parts to a zone.
    a. At the top of the zone, click **Add a Web Part.**
    b. Select the Web Part you want to add.
    c. Click **Add.**
4. If necessary, move web parts on the page by dragging them to a different location.
5. If necessary, modify web parts.
    a. From the drop-down menu near the web part, choose **Edit My Web Part.**
    b. Change the settings for the web part as needed.
    c. Click **OK.**
6. If necessary, minimize the required web part by choosing **Minimize** from the drop-down menu near the web part.
7. If necessary, hide the required web part.
    a. From the drop-down menu near the web part, choose **Edit My Web Part.**
    b. Expand **Layout**, check **Hidden** , and click **OK.**
8. If necessary, close the required web part by choosing **Close** from the drop-down menu near the web part.
9. On the Page tab, click **Stop Editing.**

Procedure Reference: Open a Closed Web Part

To open a closed Web Part:

1. Navigate to the page that contains the closed Web Part.
2. From the **Open Menu**, choose **Personalize this Page.**
3. Click **Add a Web Part.**
4. In the **Categories** section, click **Closed Web Parts.**
5. Select the web part that you want to open and click **Add.**

ACTIVITY 6-2
Personalizing Site Layout

Before You Begin

Log in to your user account **User ##.**

Scenario:

You have been told that your next assignment will entail creating a subsite for one of your projects. You decide to implement some different site layout ideas by personalizing the view of the **Our Global Company** team site.

1. Personalize the **Our Global Company** page by adding, moving, hiding, and closing **Web Parts.**

   a. On the **Quick Launch** bar, in the **Libraries** section, click the **Site Pages** link.

   b. You are logged in as **User ##.** On the **Quick Launch** bar, in the **Libraries** section, click the **Site Pages** link.

   c. On the **Site Pages - All Pages** page, from the **Open Menu** drop-down menu, choose the **Personalize this Page** option.

   d. On the **Insert** tab, in the **Web Parts** group, click **Web Part.**

   e. In the **Categories** section, verify that **Lists and Libraries** folder is selected.

   f. In **Web Parts** section, select the **Tasks** list.

   g. Click **Add.**

   h. On the **Insert** tab, in the **Web Parts** group, click **Web Part.**

   i. In the **Categories** section, select the **Social Collaboration** folder.

   j. In the **Web Parts** section, select the **User Tasks** option.

   k. Click **Add.**

l.   On the **Page** tab, in the **Edit** group, click **Stop Editing.**

2.   Switch between your personalized view and the shared view and reset your personalized view to show the default information.

a.   From the **Open Menu** drop-down menu, choose **Show Shared View.**

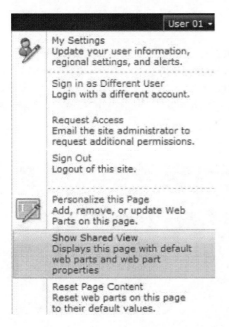

b.   Observe that the **Sites Pages - All Pages** page appears in the shared view.

c.   From the **Open Menu** drop-down menu, choose **Show Personal View** to switch back to your personalized view.

d.   Observe that the **Sites Pages - All Pages** page appears in the personal view.

e.   From the **Open Menu** drop-down menu, choose **Reset Page Content.**

f.   In the **Message from webpage** message box, click **OK.**

TOPIC C

Create an Alert

You personalized the page view by using web parts. Now, you want to send a notification about the changes made, to other site members. In this topic, you will create an alert.

With possibly hundreds of people making changes to site often in a day, it is nearly impossible to update those changes made to every document and list item. It is simply just too much information to try and monitor on your own. Instead, SharePoint alerts can notify you immediately when changes are made to the specific content you want to track.

Alerts

Definition:

An *alert* is an email notification that site content has changed. Alerts are available for any list or library in a SharePoint site. When content is changed, an email message is sent to notify the recipient of the change. Alerts can be customized to notify for all changes or a specific change based on certain criteria. The frequency of the alerts is determined when the alert is created.

Example:

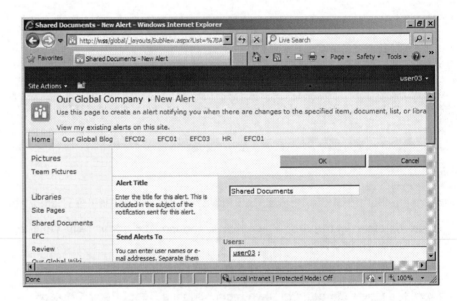

Figure 6-2: *SharePoint page for creating a new alert.*

How to Create an Alert

Procedure Reference: Create an Alert From Within the SharePoint Content

To create an alert as you view SharePoint content:

1. On the **Quick Launch** bar, click the **Tasks** link for which you want to create an alert.

2. On the **Tasks - All Tasks** page, create alert for the desired item.

    a. Select the item to create an alert.

    b. On the **Items** tab, click **Alert Me.**

    c. Choose the **Set alert on this item** option.

    d. On the **Tasks: <Task item name> – New Alert** page, in the **Alert title** text box, enter a title.

    e. In the **Send Alerts To** section, in the **Users** text box, enter user names or email addresses.

    f. In the **Delivery Method** section, observe that the **Send me alerts by e-mail** option is chosen.

    g. In the **Send Alerts for These Changes** section, under **Send me an alert when:**, observe that the **Anything Changes** option is chosen.

    h. In the **When to Send Alerts** section, observe that the **Send notification immediately** option is chosen.

    i. Click **OK.**

Procedure Reference: Manage Alerts

To manage alerts:

1. On the **Quick Launch** bar, click the **Tasks** link for which you need to create an alert.

2. On the **Tasks - All Tasks** page, select the item to create an alert.

    a. On the **Items** tab, click **Alert Me.**

    b. Choose **Manage My Alerts** option.

    c. On the **My Alerts on this Site** page, add an alert.

        a. Click the **Add Alert** link.

        b. On the **New Alert** page, from the right pane, choose the list or library option that you need to send alerts on.

        c. Click **Next.**

    d. Enter the details for creating a new alert.

    e. Click **OK.**

    f. On the **My Alerts on this Site** page, delete a selected alert.

        a. Select the necessary alert that needs to be deleted.

        b. Click the **Delete Selected Alert** link.

        c. On the **Message from webpage** message box, click **OK.**

ACTIVITY 6-3
Creating an Alert

Before You Begin:

1. Navigate to the **Our Global Company** home page.

2. Create an announcement item named **Travel Plans.**

Scenario:

Although you access the Our Global Company site several times each day, you need to know immediately when a new announcement is made on the team site. You have also been asked to keep track of the changes made on a daily basis to **Our Global Wiki** under **Our Global Company** team site.

---

1. Create an alert for the **Announcements** list.

    a. On the **Our Global Company - Home** page, on the **Quick Launch** bar, click the **Lists** link.

    b. On the **All Site Content** page, in the **Lists** section, click the **Announcements** link.

    c. On the **Announcements - All items** page, place your mouse pointer to the left of the **Travel Plans** announcement item link and check the check box that appears.

    d. On the **Items** tab, in the **Share & Track** group, click **Alert Me** and select the **Set alert on this item** option.

    e. In the **Announcements: Travel Plans - New Alert** dialog box, change the **Alert Title** to read *New Announcement!*

    f. In the **Send Alerts To** section, verify that your username is included in the **Users** text box.

    g. Verify that in the **Send Alerts for These Changes** section, **Anything changes** option is selected. And in the **When to Send Alerts** section, **Send notification immediately** option is selected.

    h. Click **OK.**

---

2. Create an alert for **Our Global Wiki.**

    a. Navigate to the **Our Global Wiki** home page.

    b. From the **Open Menu**, choose the **My Settings** option to create an alert for **Our Global Wiki.**

---

c.   On the **Personal Settings** page, click the **My Alerts** link.

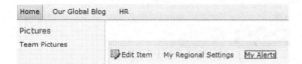

d.   On the **My Alerts on this Site** page, click the **Add Alert** link.

e.   On the **New Alert** page, in the **Choose a List or Document Library** section, select **Our Global Wiki,** click **Next.**

f.   On the **Our Global Wiki - New Alert** page, in the **Alert Title** section, change the title from **Our Global Wiki** to *Daily Changes to Our Global Wiki*

g.   In the **When to Send Alerts** section, select **Send a daily summary** and change the **Time** drop-down list to read **18:00** and click **OK.**

3.   Delete the **New Announcement!** alert for the **Our Global Company** announcement.

a.   Navigate to the **Our Global Company** team site home page.

b.   On the **Quick Launch** bar, click the **Lists** link.

c.   On the **All Site Content** page, in the **Lists** section, click the **Announcements** link.

d.   On the **Announcements - All items** page, on the **List** tab, in the **Share & Track** group, click the **Alert Me** drop-down menu and select the **Manage My Alerts** option.

e.   On the **My Alerts on this Site** page, in the **Alert Title** section, under **Frequency: Immediate** check the **New Announcement!** option.

f.   Click the **Delete Selected Alerts** link.

g.   In the **Message from webpage** message box, click **OK** to confirm the deletion of the selected alert.

TOPIC D

Subscribe to an RSS Feed

In the last topic, you created an alert. SharePoint also provides another method to notify you of content changes other than email or mobile alerts. In this topic, you will subscribe to an RSS feed.

Alerts are useful if you require summary of changes at the end of each day or on a weekly basis. For instant notification, using alerts could overload your Inbox quickly. Instead of waiting for an email to let you know when site content has changed, you can view the update immediately through an RSS feed directly from the SharePoint site.

RSS Feeds

Definition:

Really Simple Syndication (RSS) feeds are XML file formats that are used to deliver the frequently updated content of a website to any application that has feed reader capabilities. Many websites provide feeds that you can subscribe to, so that you can automatically receive updates whenever the website content is changed. The feed contains a headline and a link to the content; it can also contain a description or summary of the feed, and full or partial text from the content source.

 RSS can also stand for "Rich Site Summary." RSS feeds are sometimes referred to as web feeds, XML feeds, or often simply "feeds."

Example:

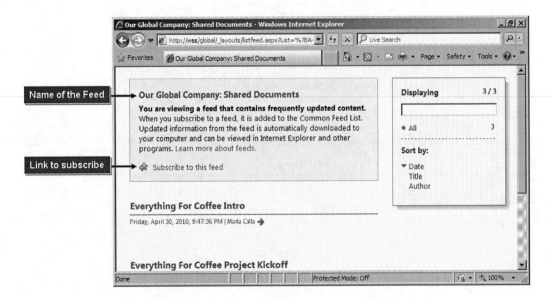

Figure 6-3: *An RSS Feed document.*

RSS Feed Support in SharePoint

In SharePoint Foundation, every list and library is automatically supplied as an RSS feed. You can view RSS feed data directly or you can display the feed data in Microsoft Outlook. RSS feeds in Outlook are created in a separate folder in the Inbox called RSS Feeds.

How to Subscribe to an RSS Feed

Procedure Reference: Subscribe to a SharePoint RSS Feed

To subscribe to a SharePoint RSS Feed:

1. Open the list or library for which you need to subscribe to an RSS Feed.
2. Select the item in the list/library items page.
3. On the **List** tab, choose **RSS Feed.**
4. In the **RSS Feed message** window, click **Subscribe to this feed.**
5. In the **Subscribe to this Feed** message window, click **Subscribe.**

Procedure Reference: View RSS Feeds in Microsoft Outlook 2010

To view RSS feeds in Microsoft Outlook 2010:

1. Open Microsoft Outlook 2010.
2. On the left pane, click **RSS Feeds.**
3. Observe that the **RSS Feeds** folder contains folders for any site to which you have subscribed.
4. Select a folder to view its RSS feeds.
5. Click a feed to view its contents.

ACTIVITY 6-4
Subscribing to an RSS Feed

Scenario:

Your manager has asked you to closely monitor any changes to Our Global Company's Tasks list. So you decide to subscribe to its RSS feed.

---

1. Subscribe to an RSS feed for the **Tasks** list on the **Our Global Company** site.

   a. On the **Quick Launch** bar, in the **Lists** section, click the **Tasks** link.

   b. On the **List** tab, in the **Share & Track** group, click **RSS Feed.**

   c. On the **Our Global Company: Tasks** page, click the **Subscribe to this feed** link.

   d. In the **Subscribe to this Feed** dialog box, click **Subscribe.**

   e. Click the **Our Global Company: Tasks** link to return to the standard SharePoint task view.

   ### Our Global Company: Tasks
   Monday, May 17, 2010, 11:52:08 PM

---

2. Confirm the creation of the RSS feed subscription.

   a. Switch to **Microsoft Outlook 2010.**

   b. On the **Microsoft Outlook** window, on the extreme left pane, expand the **RSS Feeds** folder.

   c. Observe the article related to tasks in the **Our Global Company** site.

   d. Double-click the article on the middle pane and the article opens in a new browser window. Close the browser window and Microsoft Office Outlook 2010.

Lesson 6 Follow-up

In this lesson, you customized your SharePoint environment. This will provide you with the most efficient navigation of the site content and productivity within site pages.

1. **What elements of your SharePoint environment will you customize and why?**

2. **If you create a personal page view, what will you change from the standard shared view? Why?**

7 | Creating a Team Site

Lesson Time: 2 hour(s), 20 minutes

Lesson Objectives:

In this lesson, you will create a team site.

You will:

- Create a site.
- Create a list.
- Create a library.
- Create a discussion board.
- Create a survey.

Introduction

Throughout this course, you have been working on an existing team site that contains all the team's lists, libraries, and other content. With time, as new projects are developed, you may need separate team sites to effectively manage those projects. In this lesson, you will create a team site with all the appropriate site components.

A team site can contain numerous list items and library files, with hundreds of members accessing the site daily. As more and more information is added to the site, the home page can become overloaded and difficult to navigate. Rather than add all the site content to the home page, you can organize teams, content, and members into subsites. When you create subsites to distribute the site content, members will find it easier to navigate and can stay focused on the information that pertains directly to their team.

TOPIC A
Create a Site

The first step in creating a functional tool for your team to collaborate is to create the site itself. In this topic, you will create a site.

While the team site provides a central location for everyone on the team to collaborate and share information, it may not be the best place for individual project teams to discuss specific projects or ideas that relate to a few team members. When a smaller group of individuals need a separate space to collaborate, you can create a subsite to support those collaboration efforts without providing access to everyone on the team.

Site Templates

When you create a site, you will select the site template that is appropriate for your site's needs. You can choose the desired site template from the **Template Selection** section on the **New SharePoint Site** page. Site templates are distributed in two categories namely **Collaboration** and **Meetings**. The **Collaboration** category comprises of five templates namely **Team Site, Blank Site, Blog, Document Workspace,** and **Group Work Site**. The **Meetings** category comprises of five templates namely **Group Work Site, Basic Meeting Workspace, Blank Meeting Workspace, Decision Meeting Workspace, Social Meeting Workspace,** and **Multipage Meeting Workspace**.

Template	*Used To Create*
Team Site	A central location for teams to share content, collaborate, and communicate with other team members.
Blank Site	A completely blank site with no default web parts. It can be customized to suit different requirements.
Blog	A place for a single person or a team to post ideas or thoughts and gather feedback from site visitors.
Document Workspace	A special type of site that supports team collaboration related to one specific document or meeting.
Group Work Site	A site that is a groupware solution, which allows teams to create, organize, and share information. It includes a group calendar, circulation, phone-call memo, a document library, and other basic lists.
Basic Meeting Workspace	A site for teams to plan, organize, and capture the results of a meeting. Lists for managing agendas, meeting attendees, and documents are provided along with this site.
Blank Meeting Workspace	A blank meeting site that can be customized based on user requirements.
Decision Meeting Workspace	A site that allows teams to track status or make decisions at meetings. Lists to create tasks, store documents, and record decisions are provided along with this site.

Template	Used To Create
Social Meeting Workspace	A site for teams to plan social occasions. Lists for tracking attendees, providing directions, and storing pictures are provided within this site.
Multipage Meeting Workspace	A site for teams to plan a meeting and capture the outcome of a meeting. Lists for managing the agenda and meeting attendees are provided within this site. It also provides two blank pages that can be customized.

Workspaces

A *workspace* is a SharePoint site that supports team collaboration related to one specific document or meeting. Each workspace has built-in lists and libraries to structure the information for efficient team collaboration. Your team may need to collaborate on a single document, such as a proposed budget, that does not belong in the shared library of the team site until it is approved. Team members may also need a place to keep track of budget meetings and a few related documents. These collaboration needs do not require an entirely new team site but they do need a separate and distinct location for storage and tracking. SharePoint provides several workspaces to gather this information using templates that are pre-configured with the appropriate lists and libraries.

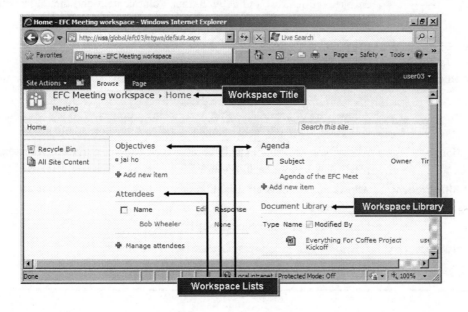

Figure 7-1: An EFC meeting workspace.

Site Creation Options

There are two ways a new site can be created:

- A site owner creates a subsite.

- Team members use Self-Service Site Creation, a feature that allows all site members to create a top-level site.

 The **Self-Service Site Creation** option is not enabled by default on a site. This option must be enabled by the site administrator.

The Site Actions Menu

The **Site Actions** menu allows site owners to create and manage all aspects of a site.

Site Actions Menu Option	Description
Edit Page	Allows you to edit, format, and align the contents of a page.
Sync to SharePoint Workspace	Allows you to synchronize the site and its contents to SharePoint Workspace, which is the new version of Microsoft Groove 2007. SharePoint Workspace enables you to work offline with SharePoint content and then update the changes once network is available.
New Page	Allows you to create a blank page that can be customized based on your requirements.
New Document Library	Allows you to create a document library to store and share your documents.
New Site	Allows you to create a site for your team or project. You can choose from a collection of available site templates for meetings or collaboration.
More Options	Allows you to create lists, libraries, pages, and sites. These options have templates that are similar to those of **New site.**
View All Site Content	Allows you to view all lists, libraries, and discussion boards of a site.
Edit in SharePoint Designer	Allows you to create and customize sites, pages, views, workflows, lists, and libraries in Microsoft SharePoint Designer.
Site Permissions	Allows you to give users access to site.
Site Settings	Provides you with access to all the settings of a site.

 Managing galleries and performing site administration and site collection administration are the advanced site owner or SharePoint administrator tasks.

How to Create a Site

Procedure Reference: Create a Subsite

To create a subsite:

1. Navigate to the site to which you want to add a subsite.
2. On the **Quick Launch** bar, click **All Site Content,** and click **Create.**
3. On the **Create** page, in the **Pages and Sites** section, click the **Team Sites** link.
4. On the **New SharePoint Site** page, specify the required details.
    1. In the **Title and Description** section, specify the desired title and description for the site.
    2. In the **Web Site Address** section, provide the URL name.
    3. In the **Template Selection** section, select the desired template.
    4. Specify whether permissions should be inherited from the parent site or unique to this subsite.
    5. Specify navigation and navigation inheritance options.
5. On the **New SharePoint Site** page, click **Create.**
6. If necessary, on the **Set Up Groups for this Site** page, configure permissions for SharePoint groups, and click **OK.**

 You will have to configure permissions for SharePoint groups only if you chose to create unique permissions for the new site in the **Permissions** section.

Procedure Reference: Add a Workspace to a Site or Subsite

To add a workspace to a site or a subsite:

1. Navigate to the site to which you want to add a workspace.
2. On the **Quick Launch** bar, click **All Site Content,** and click **Create.**
3. On the **Create** page, In the **Pages and Sites** section, click the **Sites and Workspaces** link.
4. On the **New SharePoint Site** page, fill in the required details.
    1. In the **Title and Description** section, specify the desired title and description for the site.
    2. In the **Web Site Address** section, provide the URL name.
    3. In the **Template Selection** section, select the desired worksapce template.
    4. Specify whether permissions should be inherited from the parent site or unique to this subsite.
    5. Specify navigation and navigation inheritance options.
5. Click **Create.**
6. If necessary, on the **Set Up Groups for this Site** page, configure permissions for SharePoint groups, and click **OK.**

ACTIVITY 7-1
Creating Team Sites

Before You Begin:

You have been assigned to the Site Owners group for the **Our Global Company** team site.

Scenario:

Many new projects have started recently, and your manager has requested that separate subsites be created for each project so that the **Our Global Company** team site contains information that is applicable to all employees. You decide that for the **Everything For Coffee** project, you will create a team site that nobody, but you can access until you are ready to roll it out to the rest of the team. (Team members will still be able to access the necessary information on the **Our Global Company** team site.)

1. Create a subsite named *EFC* under the **Our Global Company** team site.

    a. Scroll down the **Our Global Company** team site home page, and on the **Quick Launch** bar, click the **All Site Content** link.

    b. On the **All Site Content** page, click the **Create** link.

    c. On the **Create** page, in the **Pages and Sites** section, click the **Team Sites** link.

    d. On the **New SharePoint Site** page, in the **Title and Description** section, in the **Title** text box, type *EFC##*

    e. In the **Description** text box, type *Subsite to hold project-specific information.*

f. In the **Web Site Address** section, in the **URL name** text box, type *efc##*

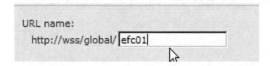

g. In the **Template Selection** section, on the **Collaboration** tab, verify that **Team Site** is selected.

h. In the **Permissions** section, under **User Permissions,** select the **Use unique permissions** option.

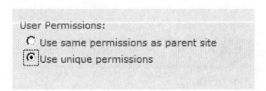

i. Observe the default settings in the **Navigation** and **Navigation Inheritance** sections. Click **Create.**

j. On the **Set Up Groups for this Site** page, verify that your name is the only one listed as a site member and a site owner, and then click **OK.**

---

2. Explore the new subsite and examine the components that it contains.

a. Examine the main page of the **EFC##** subsite.

b.   Like the **Our Global Company** main page, the **Quick Launch** bar displays a **Shared Documents** library, a **Calendar** list, a **Tasks** list, and a **Team Discussion** board. Click the **All Site Content** link.

Lists
Calendar
Tasks
EFC Team

Libraries
Site Pages
Shared Documents
Work in Progress

Discussions
Team Discussion

Surveys
EFC Site Usability
Survey

c.   In the **Lists** section, observe that only the **Announcements** list contains an item. In the **Lists** section, click the **Announcements** link.

d.   Open the announcement, **Get Started with Microsoft SharePoint Foundation!** and review its content.

e.   Click **Close.**

ACTIVITY 7-2
Creating a Workspace

Before You Begin:

You have been assigned to the Site Owners group for the **Our Global Company** team site. Give site owner permission to **mcalla** and **spretsch** for the **EFC##** subsite.

Scenario:

Now that you have a subsite for the Everything For Coffee project, you decide to take advantage of SharePoint's workspace capabilities by creating a team meeting workspace.

---

1. Create a basic meeting workspace on the EFC subsite.

   a. Navigate to **Our Global Company→EFC##.**

   b. On the ribbon, from the **Site Actions** drop-down menu, choose **More Options.**

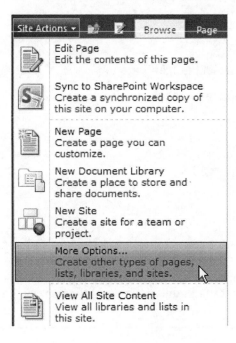

c.   On the **Create** page, in the **Pages and Sites** section, click the **Sites and Workspaces** link.

d.   On the **New SharePoint Site** page, in the **Title** text box, type *EFC Meeting Workspace*

e.   In the **Description** text box, type *Central location for EFC meeting information.*

f.   In the **Web Site Address** section, verify that the supplied part of the **URL name** reads **http://wss/global/efc##/** and then type *mtgws*

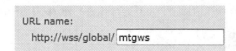

g.   In the **Template Selection** section, select the **Meetings** tab.

h.   Observe that **Basic Meeting Workspace** template is selected.

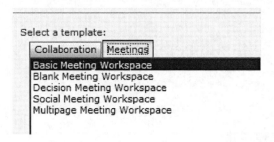

i.   Scroll down and examine the **Permissions** section. Because this workspace will be under the EFC## subsite, it can inherit the permissions you set when you created the site. Click **Create.**

2.   Explore the new workspace and add new components to it.

a.   Examine the **EFC Meeting Workspace** page.

b.   Observe that like the subsites you have been using, the **EFC Meeting Workspace** page contains several sections.

c. In the **Objectives** section, click the **Add new item** link.

d. In the **Objective** text box, type *To discuss ideas for our current project.* and click **Save.**

e. In the **Attendees** section, click the **Manage attendees** link.

f. On the **Items** tab, in the **New** group, click **New Item.**

g. In the **Attendees - New Item** dialog box, in the **Name** text box, type *Renee Baker* and click **Save.**

h. Navigate to the **EFC Meeting Workspace** home page.

i. In the **Agenda** section, click the **Add new item** link.

j. In the **Subject** text box, type *Agenda of the EFC Meeting*

k. In the **Notes** text box, type *Adopt methods to enhance the quality of the product* and click **Save.**

l. In the **Document Library** section, click the **Add document** link.

m. In the **Document Library - Upload Document** dialog box, click **Browse** and in the **Choose File to Upload** dialog box, navigate to the **C:\084696Data\Creating a Team Site** folder and select the **Everything for Coffee Project Kickoff** document.

n. Click **Open** and then click **OK.**

TOPIC B
Create a List

Your team site might require specific lists that are suitable to keep track of the information needed. In this topic, you will create unique lists suiting your needs. Your team may need additional lists, or a completely different type of list that is not available on the site by default in order to keep track of important information. In this topic, you will add a list.

Each site template has specific lists that are created when a site is created. These lists are sufficient if your team only needs to keep track of content that happens to be an announcement, calendar entry, or link. However, if, you have issues to track or specific project tasks to monitor, the default list formats are not configured for this type of information. When your team needs a different list type, as the site owner, you can add additional lists to your team site as necessary.

List Configuration Options

When you add a list to a team site, you can choose from any of the standard list types available. You will need to choose a name for the list and an optional description. You can also choose to show or hide the list title on the **Quick Launch** bar.

Meeting Workspace Lists

Meeting workspaces have unique lists that can only be added to a meeting workspace.

List Type	Description
Agenda	Provides a list of meeting topics, the presenter for each topic, and the time allotted for each.
Decisions	Tracks decisions made and meetings and shows results for attendees and other users.
Objectives	Provides objectives list for attendees prior to the meeting.
Text Box	Provides a space for custom text such as a quote or team slogan.
Things to Bring	Creates a list of items attendees should bring to a meeting.

How to Create a List

Procedure Reference: Create a List

To create a list:

1. On the Team Site page, choose **Site Actions→More Options.**

2. On the **Create** page, in the **Communications** section, click the **Contacts** link.

3. On the **New** page, in the **Name and Description** section, in the **Name** text box, type a name.

4. In the **Description** text box, type a description.

5. Click **Create.**

ACTIVITY 7-3
Creating a List

Before You Begin:

You have been assigned to the Site Owners group for the **Our Global Company** team site.

Scenario:

You are a new member of the EFC team. You decide to store the contact numbers of all your colleagues in a list to facilitate effective communication. The contact information for the team members are as follows:

- Bob Wheeler, Consultant, OGC, bwheeler@ourglobalcompany.com, 877-555-9888, 811-555-0226

- Maria Calla, Consultant, OGC, mcalla@ourglobalcompany.com, 877-555-9842, 811-555-5598

- Chou Xen Dai, Consultant, OGC, cdai@ourglobalcompany.com, 877-555-9808, 866-555-9513

- Renee Baker, Consultant, OGC, rbaker@ourglobalcompany.com, 877-555-9814, 866-555-5839

- Stefan Pretsch, Account Representative, OGC, spretsch@ourglobalcompany.com, 877-555-9837, 488-555-2886

- Takei Soto, Consultant, OGC, tsoto@ourglobalcompany.com, 877-555-9846, 488-555-7036

- Lee Prentiss, HR Systems Analyst, EFC, lprentiss@everythingforcoffee.com, 800-555-6497, 446-555-0698

- Mattias Spindler, HR Manager, EFC, mspindler@everythingforcoffee.com, 800-555-6405, 446-555-6428

---

1. On the **EFC##** subsite, create a **Contacts** list named *EFC Team*

    a. Navigate to **EFC##.**

    b. Choose **Site Actions→More Options.**

    c. On the **Create** page, in the **Communications** section, click the **Contacts** link.

    d. On the **New** page, in the **Name and Description** section, in the **Name** text box, type *EFC Team*

    e. In the **Description** text box, type *List of team members and their contact information* and click **Create.**

    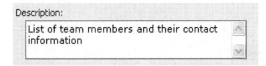

---

2. Create a list item for **Bob Wheeler.**

    a. Click the **Add new item** link.

    b. In the **EFC Team - New Item** dialog box, in the **Last Name** text box, type *Wheeler*

    c. In the **First Name** text box, type *Bob*

    d. In the **E-mail Address** text box, type *bwheeler@ourglobalcompany.com*

    e. In the **Company** text box, type *OGC*

    f. In the **Job Title** text box, type *Consultant*

    g. In the **Business Phone** text box, type *877-555-9888*

h.   In the **Mobile Number** text box, type *811-555-0226*

Last Name *	Wheeler
First Name	Bob
Full Name	
E-mail Address	bwheeler@ourglobalcompany.com
Company	
Job Title	
Business Phone	877-555-9888
Home Phone	
Mobile Number	811-555-0226

i.   Scroll down and click **Save.**

j.   Observe that the list item for Bob Wheeler is created.

Last Name	First Name	Company	Business Phone
Wheeler ☒NEW	Bob	OGC	877-555-9888

3.   Create a list item for **Lee Prentiss.**

a.   Click the **Add new item** link.

b.   In the **Last Name** text box, type *Prentiss*

c.   In the **First Name** text box, type *Lee*

d.   In the **E-mail Address** text box, type *lprentiss@everythingforcoffee.com*

e.   In the **Company** text box, type *EFC*

f.   In the **Job Title** text box, type *HR Systems Analyst*

g.   In the **Business Phone** text box, type *800-555-6497*

h.   In the **Mobile Number** text box, type *446-555-0698*

i.   Scroll down and click **Save.**

4.   Create list items for the remainder of the team.

a.   Create a list item for Maria Calla, OGC Consultant. The email address is mcalla@ourglobalcompany.com, the business phone is 877-555-9842, and the mobile phone is 811-555-5598.

b.   Create a list item for Chou Xen Dai, OGC Consultant. The email address is cdai@ourglobalcompany.com, the business phone is 877-555-9808, and the mobile phone is 866-555-9513.

c.   Create a list item for Renee Baker, OGC Consultant. The email address is rbaker@ourglobalcompany.com, the business phone is 877-555-9814, and the mobile phone is 866-555-5839.

d.   Create a list item for Stefan Pretsch, OGC Account Representative. The email address is spretsch@ourglobalcompany.com, the business phone is 877-555-9837, and the mobile phone is 488-555-2886.

e.   Create a list item for Takei Soto, OGC Consultant. The email address is tsoto@ourglobalcompany.com, the business phone is 877-555-9846, and the mobile phone is 488-555-7036.

f.   Create a list item for Mattias Spindler, EFC's HR Manager. The email address is mspindler@everythingforcoffee.com, the business phone is 800-555-6405, and the mobile phone is 446-555-6428.

TOPIC C
Create a Library

Earlier in the course you added documents to the Shared Library on a team site. Your team members may not want to store all their documents in a single library. In this topic, you will add a library.

Each team site is provided with a single default library, Shared Documents, when it is created. For smaller teams, this library may meet the document storage needs of the entire team. As the team grows, however, a single document library can become overloaded with thousands of documents and difficult to navigate. To alleviate the problem, you can add specialized libraries and organize documents, pictures, and forms into separate libraries as needed.

Library Configuration Options

Each library has specific configuration options depending on the type of library you choose.

Configuration Option	Description
Name & Description	The name of the library that will appear on the **Quick Launch** bar and an optional description of the library.
Navigation	Choose whether the library name should appear on the **Quick Launch** bar of the home page.
Document Version History	Choose whether to track each version of the document.
Document Template	Choose a document template as the default file type for new documents.

 The wiki library does not offer an option for version history and neither the wiki library nor the picture library will offer a choice of a document template.

Filter Options

Filters enable you to retrieve and display only relevant information from a library. For example, if you want to view the files modified on a particular date, you can use filters to search and display documents modified on that specified date easily and quickly.

Filter conditions enable you to show all items in a view, or display a subset of items using filters.

Condition	Applied When a Library Item
is equal to	equals a particular value.
is not equal to	is not equal to a particular value.
is greater than	is greater than a particular value.

Condition	Applied When a Library Item
is less than	is less than a particular value.
is greater than or equal to	is greater than or equal to a particular value.
is less than or equal to	is less than or equal to a particular value.
begins with	begins with a particular value.
contains	contains a particular value.

Sort Options

Sorting is the process of arranging the documents present in a library in a specific order. You can sort the documents in a document library in ascending or descending order based on their modification information. Sorting enables you to view and analyze information easily.

How to Create a Library

Procedure Reference: Create a Document Library

To add a library:

1. Navigate to the site, subsite, or workspace that will contain the new library.
2. Choose **Site Actions→More Options.**
3. On the **Create** page, in the **Libraries** section, click the **Document Library** link.
4. On the **New** page, in the **Name** text box, type a name.
5. In the **Description** text box, type a description.
6. In the **Navigation** section, specify the desired navigation option.
7. In the **Document Version History** section, specify if each version of documents in the library should be tracked.
8. In the **Document Template** section, choose **Microsoft Word document** or **Microsoft Word 97 - 2003 document**.
9. Click **Create.**

 In a similar way, you can create other libraries such as picture library and wiki library.

Procedure Reference: Require Checkout for Library Items

To require that library items be checked out for editing:

1. Navigate to the library you want to affect.
2. On the **Library** tab, in the **Settings** group, click **Library Settings.**
3. In the **General Settings** section, click **Versioning settings.**
4. In the **Require Check Out** section, click **Yes.**
5. Click **OK.**

Procedure Reference: Apply a Filter

To apply a filter:

1. Open the desired library.

2. On the **<Library name>** page, move the mouse pointer over the desired field name and from the drop-down list, select the required field to which filtering is to be applied.

3. From the **<Field name>** drop-down list, select the required item.

 To clear the filter, you can select **Clear Filter from <field name>.**

Procedure Reference: Sort the Documents in a Library

To sort the documents in a library:

1. Open the document library.

2. In the document library, click the ***<Field name>*** drop-down list to which sorting is to be done.

3. In the **<Field name>** drop-down list, select the options as required.

   - Click the **Ascending** option to sort the item in ascending order.

   - Click the **Descending** option to sort the item in descending order.

Procedure Reference: Enable Versioning for a Document Library

To enable versioning for a document library:

1. Open the document library and click the desired document or folder.

2. On the **<Library name>** page, on the **Library** tab, from the **Settings** group, click **Library Settings.**

3. On the **Document Library Settings** page, in the **General Settings** section, click the **Versioning settings** link.

4. In the **Content Approval** section, select **Yes** to enable content approval for submitted items.

5. In the **Document Version History** section, select the desired options to specify if a version needs to be created each time a file is edited in the document library.

6. In the **Draft Item Security** section, select an option to specify the users who will be able to view the drafts in the document library.

7. In the **Require Check Out** section, select the desired option to specify whether users should check out the documents before making changes in the document library.

8. Click **OK.**

Procedure Reference: View the Version History of a Document in a Document Library

To view the version history of a document:

1. On the **Quick Launch** bar, in the **Documents** section, click the desired document library.

2. From the list of documents in the library, select the desired document.

3. From the drop-down menu of the desired document, select **Version History** to view the version history of the document.

ACTIVITY 7-4
Creating a Library

Scenario:

As an end user of the EFC subsite, you decide to create a document library to store all documents specific to your team. You also decide to enable versioning and require that documents be checked out for editing since many users may access documents at the same time.

1. Create a document library named *Work in Progress* within the **EFC##** subsite. Specify that the new library should use the **Microsoft Office Word** template.

    a. Navigate to the **EFC##** subsite.

    b. On the **EFC## – Home** page, from the **Site Actions** menu, choose **More Options.**

    c. On the **Create** page, in the **Libraries** section, click the **Document Library** link.

    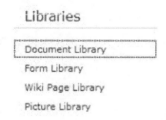

    d. On the **New** page, in the **Name** text box, type *Work in Progress*

    e. In the **Description,** type *Draft documents for the EFC project.*

    f. In the **Document Version History** section, select the **Yes** option.

    g. In the **Document Template** section, in the **Document Template** drop-down list, observe that **Microsoft Word document** is selected and click **Create.**

    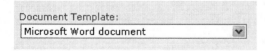

2. Ensure that the documents are checked out from the **Work in Progress** library before editing.

    a. On the **Library** tab, in the **Settings** group, click **Library Settings.**

b.   On the **Document Library Settings** page, in the **General Settings** section, click the **Versioning settings** link.

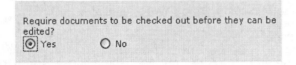

c.   On the **Document Library Versioning Settings** page, in the **Require Check Out** section, select the **Yes** option.

Require documents to be checked out before they can be edited?
◉ Yes   ○ No

d.   Click **OK.**

ACTIVITY 7-5
Organizing Documents in a Library

Data Files:

Probation Confirmation Form.doc, Employment of Relatives Policy.doc, Everything For Coffee Project Kickoff.docx

Before You Begin:

1. Navigate to the **EFC##** subsite and in the **Libraries** section, click the **Work in Progress** link.

2. Add the Probation Confirmation Form.doc, Everything For Coffee Project Kickoff.docx, and Employment of Relatives Policy.doc documents to the library at different times.

3. If necessary, switch to the **All Documents** view.

Scenario:

After the creation of the document library a collection of documents and folders has been added to it at different points in time. You decide to organize the library for effective site usage.

---

1. Filter the files in the document library.

   a. On the **EFC##** subsite, verify that the **All Documents** view is selected.

   b. On the **Work in Progress - All Documents** page, place the mouse pointer over the **Modified** field and click the drop-down arrow that appears and select the date.

   c. Verify that a filter icon appears on the side of the **Modified** field.

---

2. Sort the files in a document library.

   a. On the **Work in Progress** page, on the right-hand side of the field name **Modified,** click the drop-down option.

   b. From the **Modified** drop-down list, select **Ascending.**

---

3. Enable versioning for the **Work in Progress** library.

   a. On the **Work in Progress** page, on the **Library** tab, in the **Settings** group, click **Library Settings.**

b. On the **Document Library Settings** page, in the **General Settings** section, click the **Versioning settings** link.

c. On the **Document Library Versioning Settings** page, in the **Content Approval** section, under **Require content approval for submitted items,** select the **Yes** option.

d. In the **Document Version History** section, under **Create a version each time you edit a file in this document library,** select the **Create major and minor (draft) versions** option.

e. Scroll down to view the **Draft Item Security** section.

f. If necessary, under the **Who should see draft items in this document library** section, select **Only users who can approve items (and the author of the item).**

g. Click **OK.**

4. View the **Version History.**

a. On the **Quick Launch** bar, in the **Libraries** section, click the **Work in Progress** link.

b. Verify that the **All Documents** view is selected.

c. On the **Work in Progress - All Documents** page, place the mouse pointer over the **Everything for Coffee Project Kickoff** item and click the drop-down arrow and select **Version History.**

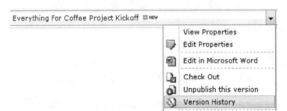

d. In the **Version History** dialog box, observe that the details of the version history being displayed.

e. Close the **Version History** dialog box.

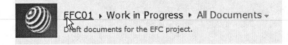

TOPIC D
Create a Discussion Board

You have created lists and libraries that help in facilitating better management of your documents to suit your organization's needs. In addition, your organization may want to use a discussion board to facilitate collaboration among team members to record views and ideas on any specific issue. In this topic, you will create a discussion board.

Several collaboration tools enable communication and sharing of critical information within an organization or a department. Discussion forum is an efficient means to facilitate discussions and information sharing. SharePoint Foundation enables you to take this forward and create discussion boards that facilitate recording and saving discussion threads within a SharePoint site.

Trigger Mails

A *trigger mail* is an email that is sent to authorized users whenever an item is posted on a discussion board. A trigger mail is also generated when a user replies to a posting or each time a discussion board item is modified.

Authorized Users

An authorized user is the one who has access to an email account and has permissions to view and post items to a discussion board in SharePoint using Microsoft Outlook.

How to Create a Discussion Board

Procedure Reference: Create a Discussion Board

To create a discussion board:

1. Display the **New** web page.
    *   Display the **New** web page using the **Site Actions** menu.
        a.   Choose **Site Actions→More Options.**
        b.   In the **Communications** section, click the **Discussion Board** link.
    *   Or, display the **New** web page using the **All Site Content** page.
        a.   On the **Quick Launch** bar, click **All Site Content.**
        b.   On the **All Site Content** web page, click **Create.**
        c.   In the **Communications** section, click the **Discussion Board** link.
2. In the **Name and Description** section, in the **Name** text box, type a name for your discussion board.
3. If necessary, in the **Description** text box, type a description of your discussion board.
4. If necessary, in the **Navigation** section, under the **Display this list on the Quick Launch** option, select **No** so that the discussion board is not displayed in the **Quick Launch** bar.
5. Click **Create** to create the new discussion board.

Procedure Reference: Add a New Discussion to a Discussion Board

To add a new discussion to a discussion board:

1. Access the desired discussion board.

2. Click the **Add new discussion** link.

3. In the **Subject** text box, type the subject of your discussion.

4. If necessary, in the **Body** text box, type the body text of your discussion.

5. If necessary, use the options on the **Edit** tab to add character and paragraph formatting to your discussion text.

6. If necessary, attach a file to your announcement.

    a. On the **Edit** tab, click **Attach File.**

    b. In the **Name** text box, enter the file path and name.

       ● Type the file name.

       ● Or, click **Browse** and in the **Choose File to Upload** dialog box, navigate to the desired folder, select the desired file, and click **Open.**

    c. Click **OK** to attach your file.

7. Click **Save** to create the discussion.

ACTIVITY 7-6
Creating a Discussion Board

Before You Begin:

1.

- ■ Log in to Windows as **User##.**
- ■ In the **Address** bar, type *http://wss/global/hr/recruitment* and press **Enter.**
- ■ You are assigned to the Site Owners group for the **Our Global Company** team site.

Scenario:

Heading the HR department, you have decided to collect and record employee views. This discussion board is required to serve as a forum to facilitate discussion among employees on the current recruitment process.

1. Create the **Suggestions##** discussion board.

   a. On the **Recruitment** subsite, from the **Site Actions** menu, choose **More Options.**

   b. In the **Communications** section, click the **Discussion Board** link.

   c. On the **New** page, in the **Name and Description** section, in the **Name** text box, type *Suggestions##*

   d. In the **Description** text box, type *Employee suggestions*, scroll down and click **Create.**

2. Add a new discussion item to the **Suggestions01** discussion board.

   a. On the **Suggestions## – Subject** page, click the **Add new discussion** link.

   b. In the **Suggestions## - New Item** dialog box, in the **Subject** text box, type *Employee Suggestions*

   c. In the **Body** text box, type *Please give your suggestions for improvement in the recruitment process.*

   d. Click **Save.**

   e. Observe that a new item with subject **Employee Suggestions** is added to the discussion board.

3. Connect to Outlook.

   a. Log on to Windows as **MCalla** in the GLOBAL domain with **!Pass1234** as the password and in the **Address** bar, type *http://wss/global/hr/recruitment* to navigate to the **Recruitment** subsite.

   b. If necessary, maximize the browser window.

   c. Navigate to the **Suggestions##** discussion board.

   d. Click the **Employee Suggestions** link.

   e. On the **List** tab, in the **Connect & Export** group, click **Connect to Outlook.**

f.   In the **Internet Explorer** dialog box, click **Allow.**

g.   In the **Microsoft Outlook** message box, click **Yes.**

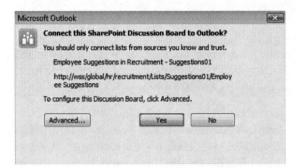

4.   Post a reply to the **Suggestions01** discussion board.

a.   If necessary, maximize the Outlook application.

b.   In the Outlook application, expand the **SharePoint Lists** folder, and click **Recruitment – Suggestions##.**

c.   Double-click the mail with the subject **Employee Suggestions.**

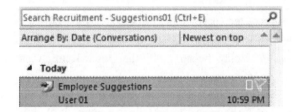

d.   On the **Discussion** tab, in the **Respond** group, click **Post Reply.**

e.   In the text area, type *We should hire more folks this Fall.* and click **Post.**

f.   Close the **Employee Suggestions - Discussion** discussion item window.

g.   Close the Outlook application.

5.   Ensure that the reply is posted in the SharePoint site.

a.   Refresh the browser window.

b.   On the **Employee Suggestions - Flat** page, observe the reply for the **Employee Suggestions** email.

c.   Navigate to the **HR** subsite's home page.

TOPIC E
Create a Survey

Throughout the course, you and your team have freely contributed information to lists, libraries, blogs, wikis, and discussion boards. Now you want to gather information from team members based on responses to specific questions. In this topic, you will create a survey.

One thing you can always count on in any organization is that data will need to be summarized and reports generated. Summary data can be an invaluable source of information for managers and survey results can provide valuable feedback on a wide range of subjects. As a site owner, you can create surveys and gather feedback from site users or everyone with access to the team site. When the feedback is summarized in a structured format, it is easy to scan for relevant information.

Survey Configuration Options

A survey has numerous configuration options available.

Option	*Description*
Name and Description	Specifies the name of the survey that will appear on the **Quick Launch** bar and an optional description.
Navigation	Decides whether to display the survey on the **Quick Launch** bar of the home page.
Survey Options	Specifies options to show the name of survey respondents on the results page and/or to allow respondents to take the survey multiple times.
Question and Type	Enters a survey question and the format for the answer. The question types are generally self-explanatory and provide a range of response options, including free-form text and multiple choice.
Additional Question Settings	Chooses additional options based on the type of answer allowed.
Branching Logic	Specifies if an answer to a question will trigger more questions based on the answer.

limit options
open ended questions (Predictable responses)

How to Create a Survey

Procedure Reference: Create a Survey

To create a survey:

1. Navigate to the site, subsite, or workspace that will contain the new survey.

2. Choose **Site Actions→More Options,** and on the **Create** page, click **Survey.**

3. On the right pane, click **More Options,** enter a **Name** and **Description.**

4. In the **Navigation** section, indicate whether or not the survey should be displayed on the **Quick Launch** bar.

5. In the **Survey Options** section, specify whether to show user names in the survey results and whether to allow users to respond more than once. Click **Create.**

6. On the **New Question** page, enter a **Question** and select the **Question Type.**

7. Complete the **Additional Question Settings** section as required.

8. If you need to add more survey questions, click **Next Question;** otherwise, click **Finish.**

9. Complete the **New Question** page as many times as is needed to include all of your survey questions, and then click **Finish.**

10. If necessary, on the **Customize** page, click a survey question to add branching logic to the question.

11. If necessary, click **Change the order of the questions** to reorder the questions.

Procedure Reference: Respond to a Survey

To respond to a survey:

1. Navigate to the survey that you want to take, click **Respond to this Survey,** and provide your answers.

2. If necessary, click **Save** to save your responses without completing the survey, or click **Next,** and answer the remaining questions.

3. Click **Finish.**

Procedure Reference: View Survey Responses

To view responses to a survey:

1. Navigate to the survey that contains the responses that you want to view.

2. The **Overview** view is displayed by default. You can display responses in a text-based or graphical format.

3. If necessary, display the text-based response format.

    a. Click **Show all responses,** or from the **View** drop-down menu, choose **All Responses.**

    b. Click a response. You can create, edit, or delete responses, manage permissions, and create alerts from this page.

    c. When you have finished working with the response, click **Close.**

4. If necessary, to display the graphical response format, click **Show a graphical summary of responses,** or from the **View** drop-down menu, choose **Graphical Summary.**

ACTIVITY 7-7
Creating a Survey

Before You Begin:

You are assigned to the Site Owners group for the **EFC##** subsite.

Scenario:

You have decided to ask other EFC teammates their opinions on the usability of the **EFC01** subsite.

---

1. Create a survey called **EFC Site Usability Survey.**

   a. Navigate to **EFC##** site.

   b. On the **EFC## - Home** page, from the **Site Actions** menu, choose **More Options.**

   c. On the **Create** page, in the **Tracking** section, click the **Survey** link.

   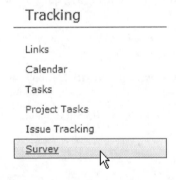

   d. On the **New** page, in the **Name and Description** section, in the **Name** text box, type **EFC Site Usability Survey**

   e. In the **Description** text box, type **To gather information about possible improvements to the EFC site.**

   f. In the **Survey Options** section, for **Allow multiple responses,** select the **Yes** option and click **Next.**

   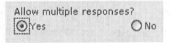

---

2. Add a question that provides a menu of choices to participants.

   a. On the **New Question** page, in the **Question and Type** section, in the **Question** text box, type **How easy is it to find information on the EFC site?**

   b. Verify that the **Choice (menu to choose from)** option is selected.

c.   In the **Additional Question Settings** section, select the text in the **Type each choice on a separate line** text box, type *Very easy* and press **Enter.**

d.   Type *Somewhat easy* and press **Enter.**

e.   Type *Neither easy nor difficult* and press **Enter.**

f.   Type *Somewhat difficult* and press **Enter.**

g.   Type *Very difficult*

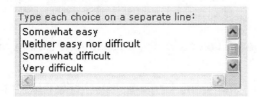

h.   Click **Next Question.**

---

3.   Add questions that provide a single-line text box and a multiple-line text box for participants to type their responses.

a.   In the **Question and Type** section, in the **Question** text box, type *What type of information do you access most often?*

b.   Under **The type of answer to this question is**, select the **Single line of text** option.

c.   Observe that the **Additional Question Settings** section changes to reflect the question type that you selected. Click **Next Question.**

d.   In the **Question** text box, type *What should be added to the EFC site?*

e.   Under **The type of answer to this question is**, select the **Multiple lines of text** option.

f.   Scroll down and in the **Additional Question Settings** section, in the **Number of lines for editing** text box, select the number and type *10*

g.   Click **Next Question.**

h.   In the **Question** text box, type *What suggestions do you have for improving the EFC site?*

i.   Select the **Multiple lines of text** option.

j.   In the **Number of lines for editing** text box, select the number and type *10*

k.   Select the **Enhanced rich text (Rich text with pictures, tables, and hyperlinks)** option.

l.   Click **Next Question.**

---

4.   Add questions that ask participants to respond either Yes or No.

a.   In the **Question** text box, type *Do you have any suggestions for improving the usability of this site?*

b.   Select the **Yes/No (check box)** option.

c.   Click **Next Question.**

> d.   In the **Question** text box, type *Are you willing to help implement future site improvements?*
>
> e.   Select the **Yes/No (check box)** option.
>
> f.   In the **Additional Question Settings** section, from the **Default value** drop-down list, select **No.**
>
> g.   Click **Finish.**

5.   Add branching logic to a question.

   a.   In the **Questions** section, click the **Do you have any suggestions for improving the usability of this site?** link.

   b.   On the **Edit Question** page, in the **Branching Logic** section, verify that for the **Yes** drop-down list, **No Branching** is selected.

   c.   From the **No** drop-down list, select **Are you willing to help implement future site improvements?**

   d.   Click **OK.**

6.   Rearrange the order of the questions.

   a.   Click the **Change the order of the questions** link.

   b.   For the **What suggestions do you have for improving the EFC site** question name, set **Position from Top** to **5.**

   c.   Click **OK.**

   d.   Observe that the order of questions have changed.

   e.   On the **Top-Links** bar, click the **EFC##** tab to navigate to the **EFC##** home page.

PRACTICE ACTIVITY 7-8
Testing the Survey

Scenario:

Once you have created the survey, you will need to test the branching logic and verify that you can view the responses.

1. Take the survey twice to test the branching logic.

2. View the survey responses in both text-based and graphical formats.

Lesson 7 Follow-up

In this lesson, you created a team site. Rather than adding all site content to a single home page, you can organize the content into subsites. When you distribute the site content over several subsites, members will find it easier to navigate and can stay focused on the information that pertains directly to their team.

1. **When you create a new team site, will you use the default lists and libraries on the site or will you add your own? If so, which lists or libraries will you add?**

2. **In your environment, will you use document and meeting workspaces? If so, what will you use them for?**

8 | Performing Basic Site Administration

Lesson Time: 1 hour(s)

Lesson Objectives:

In this lesson, you will perform basic site administration.

You will:

- Grant access to a site.
- Manage site look and feel.

Introduction

In the last lesson, you created a site. Now as the site owner, you need to perform the daily tasks that keep the site running efficiently. In this lesson, you will perform basic site administration.

In almost every organization, network and email administrators perform daily tasks to keep the system accessible to the appropriate individuals and available whenever the resources are needed. As a SharePoint site owner, you will be responsible for performing similar tasks to ensure the availability of site content and provide site visitors and site members access to the resources they need.

TOPIC A
Manage Users and Groups

In the previous lesson, you have created a site and added the appropriate lists, libraries, and views necessary for your team. Now you need to make the site available to team members and visitors. As new individuals join the team and others leave, you will also need to modify access to your site accordingly. In this topic, you will grant access to a SharePoint site and manage users and group.

You created a SharePoint site. A host of new users have joined the site. By granting access to team members, your site will become more robust as team members add content and collaborate with each other. Over time, the level of access each group possess may need to change, or you may need to create an entirely new group with specific access rights. As the site owner, you can create, modify, and delete groups as necessary to ensure team members and visitors have the appropriate access to your site.

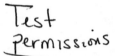

Site Access Permissions

As a site owner, you can grant access to a site through one of the three default SharePoint groups, or you can add the user to the SharePoint site directly and assign individual permissions based on the user's role.

Permission	Description
Full Control	Permits unlimited control of an entire site, including content and access control.
Limited Access	Permits access to shared resources in a site and also items within a site. Designed to grant users unique categorical access to a specific list, library, item, or document, without giving users access to the entire site.
Design	Enables users to view, add, update, delete, approve, and also customize site content.
Contribute	Enables users to only view, add, update, and delete site content.
Read	Limits users to viewing only the content.

User and Group Management Tasks

Common SharePoint user and group management tasks that you will need to perform as a site owner include:

- Creating groups
- Changing group memberships
- Modifying a group's settings
- Deleting groups
- Deciding the groups that should appear on the **People and Groups Quick Launch.**

How to Manage Users and Groups

Procedure Reference: Grant Access to a Site

To grant access to a site:

1. Navigate to the desired site and choose **Site Actions→Site Settings.**

2. In the **Users and Permissions** section, click **People and groups.**

3. On the **People and Groups: <sitename> Members** page, click **New.**

4. In the **Add Users** section, either type the user names, or use the **Browse** button to select the names from the directory.

5. In the **Give Permissions** section, select either **Add users to a SharePoint group** or **Give users permission directly.**

    *   If you select **Add users to a SharePoint group,** provide the name of the SharePoint group.

    *   If you select **Give users permission directly,** select the permissions that the users should be assigned.

6. In the **Send Email** section, check or uncheck the **Send welcome e-mail to the new users** check box. If you want to include a personal message, type the message in the **Personal Message** text box.

7. Click **OK.**

Procedure Reference: Grant Access to a List

To grant access to a list:

1. Open the list that you want to affect.

2. On the **<List>** tab, in the **Settings** group, click **List Settings.**

3. On the **List Settings** page, in the **Permissions and Management** column, click **Permissions for this list.**

4. Modify the permission level of an existing user's or group's permissions. and

    1. Select a user or group.

    2. On the **Edit** tab, in the **Modify** group, click **Edit User Permissions.**

    3. In the **Edit Permissions** dialog box, choose the desired permission level and click **OK.**

5. Prevent a user or a group from accessing the site.

    1. Select a user or group.

    2. On the **Edit** tab, in the **Modify** group, click **Remove User Permissions.**

    3. In the **Message from webpage** message box, click **OK** to confirm preventing the user/group from accessing the site.

6. To add permissions for another user or group, on the **Edit** tab, in the **Grant** group, click **Grant Permissions,** add the user or users, configure the permissions, provide a personal email message, and click **OK.**

Granting Access to Libraries and Other Site Content

Granting access to libraries and other site content is similar to granting access to a list, but some of the menu choices will be slightly different.

Procedure Reference: Create a SharePoint Group for a Site

To create a SharePoint group for a site:

1. Choose **Site Actions→Site Settings.**
2. In the **Users and Permissions** section, click **People and groups.**
3. On the Quick Launch bar, click **Groups.**
4. On the **People and Groups** page, choose **New→New Group** to add a new group.
5. On the **Create Group** page, in the **Name and About Me Description** section, in the **Name** text box, enter a name for the group.
6. If necessary, in the **About Me** text box, enter a description for the SharePoint group.
7. In the **Owner** section, in the Group Owner text box, specify the user or group responsible for the new group.
8. If necessary, in the **Group Settings** section:
   a. Select an option to view the membership for this group.
   b. Select an option to edit membership for this group.
9. If necessary, in the **Membership Requests** section:
   a. Select an option to allow members to join or leave this group.
   b. Select an option to accept members for this group automatically.
10. In the **Give Group Permission to this Site** section, choose the desired permission level.
11. Click **Create.**

Procedure Reference: Adjust a SharePoint Group's Membership

To adjust a SharePoint Group's Membership:

1. Choose **Site Actions→Site Settings.**
2. In the **Users and Permissions** section, click **People and groups.**
3. On the **Quick Launch** bar, click **Groups.**
4. In the **Group** column, click the group that you want to modify.
5. Add users to the group.
   a. Choose **New→Add Users.**
   b. Browse for and select, or type the names of users to be added to the group.
   c. If necessary, type an email message for the new user.
   d. Click **OK.**
6. Remove users from the group.
   a. Check the check boxes next to the users to be removed from the group.
   b. Choose **Actions→Remove Users from Group.**
   c. In the **Message from webpage** message box, click **OK.**

Procedure Reference: Change a SharePoint Group's Settings

To change a SharePoint group's settings:

1. Choose **Site Actions→Site Settings.**
2. In the **Users and Permissions** section, click **People and groups.**
3. On the **Quick Launch** bar, click **Groups** to view all the groups.
4. In the **Group** column, click the edit button next to the group that you want to modify.

5.   On the **Change Group Settings** page, adjust the settings as necessary:

    a.   If necessary, in the **Name and About Me** Section, in the **Name** text box, or, **Description** text box, replace the existing text with a new name or description.

    b.   If necessary, in the **Owner** section, in the **Group Owner** text box, change the group owner.

    c.   If necessary, in the **Group Settings** section, change the group settings.

    d.   If necessary, in the **Membership Requests** section, select new options.

6.   To delete a setting:

    1.   Click **Delete.**

    2.   On the message window, click **OK.**

7.   Click **OK.**

Procedure Reference: Edit the Groups Quick Launch List

To edit the groups in the Quick Launch list:

1.   On the **Team site** home page, choose **Site Actions→Site Settings.**

2.   In the **Users and Permissions** section, click **People and groups.**

3.   On the **Quick Launch** bar, click **Groups** to view all the groups.

4.   Choose **Settings→Edit Group Quick Launch.**

5.   Modify the **Groups** section to include the SharePoint groups that should be displayed.

6.   Click **OK.**

ACTIVITY 8-1
Granting Access to a Site

Before You Begin:

1. Log in to your user account **User##**.

2. Navigate to the **EFC##** home page.

3. You are assigned to the Site Owners group for the **EFC##** subsite.

Scenario:

You are ready to roll out the EFC site to the team. You need to be sure that all EFC team members can access the site's content. You also must ensure that users from other teams will not be able to access the site because the site may contain confidential information.

---

1. Add **Our Global Company** employees to the **EFC## Members** group.

    a.   As **User##,** on the **EFC## – Home** page, choose **Site Actions→Site Settings.**

    b.   On the **Site Settings** page, in the **Users and Permissions** section, click the **People and groups** link.

    c.   On the **People and groups** page, click **New.**

    d.   In the **Grant Permissions** dialog box, in the **Select Users** section, click the **Browse** icon.

    e.   In the **Select People and Groups – – Webpage Dialog** dialog box, in the **Find** text box, type *wheeler* and press **Enter.**

Find	wheeler				🔎
Display Name	Title	Department	E-Mail		Mobile
Bob W	Senior Consultant	Client Services	bwheeler@ourglobalcompany.com		

    f.   Select **Bob Wheeler** and click **Add.**

    g.   Click **OK.**

    h.   Use this method to add **Chou Xen Dai, Renee Baker, Stefan Pretsch** and **Takei Soto** to the **Select Users** text box.

    i.   In the **Grant Permissions** dialog box, in the **Send E-Mail** section, in the **Personal Message** text box, type *Welcome! I'm the site owner, so let me know if you have any questions or comments. Thanks.*

    j.   Click **OK.**

    k.   From the **Settings** drop-down list, select **View Group Permissions** to verify that the permissions level of **EFC##** members is **Contribute.**

    l.   Observe that the permission level of **EFC##** members is **Contribute.** and click **OK.**

    m.   Return to the **EFC##** subsite.

2. Test access to the **EFC##** site by logging in as a user who do not have access.

    a. From the **Open Menu** menu, choose **Sign in as Different User.**

    b. Connect to the SharePoint server with the **User name** *GLOBAL\schandler* and the **Password** *!Pass1234.*

ACTIVITY 8-2
Managing Users and Groups

Before You Begin:

1. You are assigned to the Site Owners group for the **EFC##** subsite.

2. Log in to your user account **User##.**

Scenario:

Several personnel and assignment changes have occurred at **Our Global Company.**

- Renee Baker has been transferred and will no longer be actively involved in the EFC project, but she has been asked to monitor the progress of the project.

- Takei Soto has been promoted to Senior Consultant, and you have been asked to be a mentor, while Soto will be assisting you with the site-ownership tasks for the EFC subsite.

You as a manager, now decide that this would be an ideal time to adjust the **Quick Launch** bar so that it displays only the EFC groups.

---

1. Remove **Renee Baker** from the **EFC## Members** group.

    a. On the **EFC## – Home** page, choose **Site Actions→Site Settings.**

    b. On the **Site Settings** page, in the **Users and Permissions** section, click the **People and groups** link.

    c. On the **People and Groups** page, check the check box next to **Renee Baker.**

        Renee Baker

    d. Choose **Actions→Remove Users from Group.**

    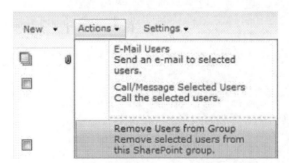

    e. In the **Message from webpage** message box, click **OK.**

---

2. Create the **EFC## Visitors** group and add **Renee Baker** to it.

---

a. On the **Quick Launch** bar, click the **Groups** link.

b. On the **People and Groups: All Groups** page, from the **New** drop-down menu, choose **New Group.**

c. In the **Name and About Me Description** section, in the **Name** text box, type *EFC ## Visitors*

d. In the **About Me** text box, click and type *People with read permissions for the EFC## subsite.*

e. In the **Group Settings** section, verify that only the group owner can edit the membership of the group.

f. Scroll down and click **Create.** On the **People and Groups** page, click **New.**

g. In the **Grant Permissions** dialog box, in the **Select Users** section, in the **Users/Groups** text box, type *Renee Baker* and click the **Check Names** icon.

h. Click **OK.**

---

3. Add **Takei Soto** to the **EFC## Owners** group.

a. On the **Quick Launch** bar, click the **Groups** link.

b. Click **EFC## Owners** and then click **New.**

c. In the **Grant Permissions** dialog box, in the **Select Users** section, in the **Users/Groups** text box, type *Takei Soto.*

d. Click the **Check Names** icon to browse for and add **Takei Soto** in the **Users/Groups** text box.

e. Click **OK.**

---

4. Remove the **Team Site Visitors** group from the **Quick Launch** bar.

a. On the **Quick Launch** bar, click the **Groups** link.

b. On the **People and Groups: All Groups** page, from the **Settings** drop-down menu, choose **Edit Group Quick Launch.**

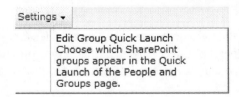

c. On the **Edit Group Quick Launch** page, in the **Groups** text box, select **Team Site Visitors;** and press **Delete.** Click **OK.**

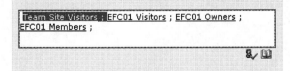

TOPIC B
Manage Site Look and Feel

In a previous topic, you customized your own SharePoint environment. As the site owner, you now want to make global customization for the entire site. In this topic, you will manage the look and feel of the team site.

All sites and workspaces are created from the same templates and look exactly the same, with the exception of the title and web address. If nothing ever changed on the site except the content, it would be difficult to quickly see the difference from site to site. By changing the graphics, colors, and layout of a site, you make it unique and easily distinguishable from other sites.

Site Graphics

There are two primary graphics that can be modified by a site owner on a team site.

Graphic	Description
Site icon	Located in the upper left corner, next to the site title. The site icon appears on each page in the site.
Site image	It is an image web part. It is located in the upper right corner of the home page by default but like other web parts, it can be moved anywhere on the page.

 Other graphics that appear on site pages require web design tools to make modifications.

Site Themes

Each page in a SharePoint site is created with the default theme. The theme determines the colors and fonts used throughout the site but does not affect subsites. SharePoint provides several different pre-built themes and the site theme can be changed at any time, as often as needed.

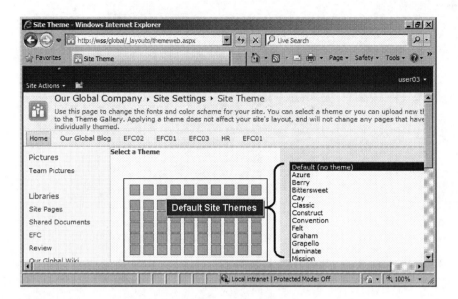

Figure 8-1: *The Site Theme page.*

 Any pages in a site that have been customized with a web design tool are not affected by changing the site theme.

The Tree View Tool

Definition:

Tree View is a navigation tool that displays the content of a SharePoint site in a hierarchy rather than a list. A site owner can choose to enable tree view alone or in addition to the **Quick Launch** bar. When tree view is enabled, all site content appears in a format similar to Windows explorer with each site grouped with its own subsites, lists, and libraries. Items in tree view can be expanded or collapsed, depending on the level of detail desired.

Example:

Figure 8-2: A Tree View.

Navigation Customizations

The navigation in a SharePoint site can be customized so the names of lists, libraries, and sites appear exactly the way you want.

Tool	Options
Quick Launch	Add, delete, and reorder list, library, and site names as well as headings on the **Quick Launch.**
Top link bar	Add, delete, and reorder site names that appear in the top link bar.
Tree view	Enable hierarchical view (similar to Windows explorer) to use in addition to the **Quick Launch** bar or as a replacement for the **Quick Launch** bar.

How to Manage Site Look and Feel

Procedure Reference: Change a Site's Title, Description, or Icon

To change a site's title, description, or icon:

1. Navigate to the site that you want to customize.

2. Choose **Site Actions→Site Settings.**

3. In the **Look and Feel** section, click **Title, description, and icon.**

4. On the **Title, Description, and Icon** page, in the **Title and Description** section, in the **Title** text box, replace the text in the **Title** text box to change the title.

5. In the **Description** text box, replace the text to change the site's description.

6. In the **Logo URL and Description** section, in the **URL** text box, enter the link to access the logo image file.

7. In the **Enter a description** text box, enter a short description of the image.

8. Click **OK.**

Procedure Reference: Change the Site Theme

To change the site theme:

1. Navigate to the site that you want to affect.

2. Choose **Site Actions→Site Settings.**

3. In **Look and Feel** section, click **Site theme.**

4. On the **Site Theme** page, select a theme.

5. Click **Apply.**

Procedure Reference: Change Site Navigation Tools

To change site navigation tools:

1. Navigate to the site that you want to affect.

2. Choose **Site Actions→Site Settings.**

3. If necessary, disable the **Quick Launch** bar.

   a. On the **Site Settings** page, in **Look and Feel** section, click **Tree view.**

   b. Uncheck the **Enable Quick Launch** check box.

   c. Click **OK.**

4. If necessary, enable the **Tree view.**

   a. On the **Site Settings** page, in the **Look and Feel** section, click **Tree view.**

   b. Check **Enable Tree View.**

   c. Click **OK.**

5. If necessary, under **Look and Feel,** click **Top link bar.**

   - If the site inherits Top Link bar links from its parent site, then click **Stop Inheriting Links.**

   - If the site does not inherit Top Link bar links from the parent site, and you want to create new links, click **New Navigation Link,** enter a web address and description, and click **OK.**

   - If the site does not inherit Top Link bar links from the parent site, and you want to use the links from the parent site, click **Use Links from Parent** and in the **Message from webpage** message box, click **OK.**

6. If necessary, change the **Quick Launch** bar.

    a. In the **Look and Feel** section, click **Quick launch.**

    b. On the **Quick Launch** page, click the **New Navigation Link** link.

    c. On the **New Navigation Link** page, provide the web address, description, and heading, and then click **OK** to add links.

    d. To add headings, click **New Heading,** provide the web address and description, and click **OK.**

    e. To rearrange the elements in the **Quick Launch** bar, click **Change Order,** use the drop-down lists to select a new order for the links, and click **OK.**

Procedure Reference: Manage Shared Web Parts

To manage shared Web Parts:

1. Navigate to the site that you want to modify.

2. Choose **Site Actions→Edit Page.**

3. For the shared web part that you want to modify, click the drop-down arrow and select **Edit Web Part.**

4. In the **<Web part title>** tool box, change the settings as necessary and click **Apply** and **OK.**

5. On the **Format Text** tab, click the **Save & Close** button.

ACTIVITY 8-3
Changing the Site Look and Feel

Data Files:

ogclogo.jpg, efclogo.jpg

Before You Begin:

1. Navigate to the **EFC##** subsite home page.

2. You have been assigned to the site owners group for the **EFC##** subsite.

Scenario:

You have been given permission to modify the EFC subsite's appearance, as long as the necessary information remains available to team members. You decide to change the site appearance to:

- Enable the Tree View navigation element.

- Include the Our Global Company and EFC logos (ogclogo.jpg and efclogo.jpg) on the site.

- Change the site theme to Ricasso.

- Revise the EFC home page to replace the Shared Documents library with the EFC Team list.

● Rearrange the Quick Launch bar to show site content in the following order:

■ Lists

■ Libraries

■ Discussions

■ Surveys

1. Upload the logo files to the **Shared Documents** library of the **EFC##** subsite.

a. On the **EFC## – Home** page, on the **Quick Launch** bar, in the **Libraries** section, click the **Shared Documents** link.

b. On the **Shared Documents - All Documents** page, on the **Documents** tab, in the **New** group, from the **Upload Document** drop-down menu, choose **Upload Multiple Documents.**

c. In the **Shared Documents - Upload Multiple Documents** dialog box, click the **Browse for files instead** link.

d. Navigate to C:\084696Data\Performing Basic Site Administration. In the **Open** dialog box, double-click the **Performing Basic Site Administration** folder to navigate to the required files. Select the **efclogo.jpg** and **ogclogo.jpg** files and click **Open.**

e. Click **OK.**

f. Click **Done.**

2. Add **ogclogo.jpg** as the **EFC##** subsite logo.

a. On the **Shared Documents - All Documents** page, click the **ogclogo** file item link.

b. In the **Open Document** message box, click **OK.**

c. In the browser window, in the **Address** bar, right-click and choose **Copy** to copy it to the clipboard.

d. Click the browser's **Back** button.

e. On the **Shared Documents - All Documents** page, from the **Site Actions** drop-down menu, choose **Site Settings.**

f. On the **Site Settings** page, in the **Look and Feel** section, click the **Title, description, and icon** link.

g. On the **Title, Description and Icon** page, in the **Logo URL and Description** section, in the **URL** text box, click and paste the contents of the Clipboard.

h. Click the **Click here to test** link.

i. Observe that the logo is displayed in a new browser window. Close the new browser window.

j. In the **Enter a description (used as alternative text for the picture)** text box, click and type *Our Global Company logo*

k. On the **Title, Description and Icon** page, click **OK.**

l. On the **Site Settings** page, observe that the logo is displayed before **EFC##** → **Site Settings.**

3. Change the site theme to **Ricasso.**

   a. On the **Site Settings** page, in the **Look and Feel** section, click the **Site theme** link.

   b. On the **Site Theme** page, in the list box, select **Ricasso.**

   c. Click **Apply.**

4. Enable the **Tree view** navigation element.

   a. On the **Site Settings** page, in the **Look and Feel** section, click the **Tree view** link.

   b. On the **Tree view** page, in the **Enable Tree View** section, check the **Enable Tree View** option.

   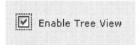

   c. Click **OK.**

   d. On the **Quick Launch** bar, observe that contents of the site are display in tree view.

   e. Navigate to the **EFC##** subsite home page.

5. Rearrange the **Quick Launch** bar.

   a. On the **EFC01 – Home** page, from the **Site Actions** drop-down menu, choose the **Site Settings** option.

   b. On the **Site Settings** page, in the **Look and Feel** section, click the **Quick launch** link.

   c. On the **Quick Launch** page, click the **Change Order** link.

   d. In the **Lists** section, from the ordering drop-down list, select **1** to place **Lists** in the first position.

   e. In the **Libraries** section, from the ordering drop-down list, select **2** to place **Libraries** in the second position.

   f. In the **Discussions** section, from the ordering drop-down list, select **3** to place **Discussions** in the third position.

   g. Verify that **Surveys** is placed in the fourth position and click **OK.**

   h. On the **Quick Launch** bar, observe that the order of the contents has changed.

   i. Navigate to **Team Site** → **Our Global Company** → **EFC##** subsite.

6. On the **EFC##** home page, replace the **Shared Documents** library with the **EFC Team** list.

   a. On the **EFC## – Home** page, choose **Site Actions→Edit Page.**

   b. Click the **Shared Documents** drop-down arrow, select **Delete.**

   c. In the **Message from webpage** message box, click **OK.**

   d. On the **Insert** tab, in the **Web Parts** group, click **Web Part.**

   e. In the **Web Parts** section. select **EFC Team** and click **Add.**

   f. On the ribbon, on the **Format Text** tab, click the **Save & Close** button.

7. Modify the **Site Image** web part to show **efclogo.jpg.**

   a. On the **EFC## - Home** page, on the **Quick Launch** bar, in the **Libraries** section, click the **Shared Documents** link.

   b. On the **Shared Documents - All Documents** page, click the **efclogo** link.

   c. In the **Open Document** message box, click **OK.**

   d. Select the text in the **Address** bar and copy it to the Clipboard.

   e. Click the browser's **Back** button.

   f. Return to the **EFC##** home page.

   g. On the **EFC## – Home** page, choose **Site Actions→Edit Page.**

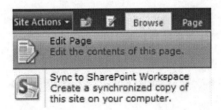

   h. On the **Insert** tab, in the **Media** group, choose **Picture → From Address.**

   i. In the **Select Picture** dialog box, in the **Address** text box, paste the contents of the clipboard. In the **Alternative Text** text box, click and type *EFC's logo*

   j. Click **OK.**

   k. On the ribbon, on the **Format Text** tab, click the **Save & Close** button.

   l. Observe that the **Site Image** logo has been replaced.

   m. Navigate to the **Our Global Company** home page.

Lesson 8 Follow-up

In this lesson, you performed basic site administration tasks to manage users, site layout, and site content. By performing daily administrative tasks in your site, you will ensure team members have the appropriate access to site resources and the site is easy to navigate.

1. **When you add users to your SharePoint site, will you add them to one of the three default groups or will you create a new group? If you create a new group, what rights will you assign that group and why?**

2. **On your team site, will you modify the appearance of any elements? If so, which elements would you modify and why?**

Follow-up

In this course, you created and edited content in a Microsoft SharePoint Foundation team site, and then you created and managed your own team site. By implementing and using Microsoft SharePoint Foundation, you can leverage the power and flexibility of one of the most sophisticated software tools for team collaboration available today and create a collaborative environment that promotes team productivity and efficiency.

1. **How will you and your team use a SharePoint site in your organization?**

2. **What features of Microsoft SharePoint Foundation will you use the most? Are there features you will not use?**

3. **If you are responsible for managing a site, what site owner tasks will you perform most often?**

What's Next?

Microsoft® SharePoint® Foundation 2010: Level 1 is the first course in a two part series. The next course, *Microsoft® SharePoint® Foundation 2010: Level 2*, builds on the Level 1 course and focuses on advanced site owner and introductory SharePoint Administrator functions including content management, customization of site content and layout, permissions and access rights, and site collection management.

Lesson Labs

Lesson labs are provided as an additional learning resource for this course. The labs may or may not be performed as part of the classroom activities. Your instructor will consider setup issues, classroom timing issues, and instructional needs to determine which labs are appropriate for you to perform, and at what point during the class. If you do not perform the labs in class, your instructor can tell you if you can perform them independently as self-study, and if there are any special setup requirements.

Lesson 2 Lab 1

Working with Lists

Activity Time: 35 minutes

Scenario:

As an employee of Our Global Company, you have various types of information to share with your team members on the default SharePoint Team Site. In particular, you want to practice working with lists.

1. On the **Team Site,** create several list items in the default lists.

 Be sure you are working in the **Team Site** and not the **Our Global Company** subsite when performing the lab activities.

2. On the **Team Site,** investigate the various views available for default lists.

3. On the **Team Site,** create one or more personal views.

Lesson 3 Lab 1

Working with Libraries

Activity Time: 40 minutes

Scenario:

You are an employee at **Our Global Company.** Your manager has asked you to share relevant documents contextual to your project via your team site. In particular, you want to practice working with libraries.

1.   On the team site, create at least three documents in the **Shared Documents** library.

2.   On the team site, create a personal view for the **Shared Documents** library.

3.   On the team site, delete at least two documents from the **Shared Documents** library.

4.   On the team site, open the **Recycle Bin.** Permanently delete one document, and restore another to the **Shared Documents** library.

5.   Create a folder in the **Shared Documents** library.

Lesson 4 Lab 1
Communicating with Team Members

Activity Time: 55 minutes

Scenario:

As an employee of Our Global Company, you will be using SharePoint for various types of team communication. You want to practice communicating with team members through the SharePoint interface.

1.   On the **Team Site,** on the **Team Discussion** page, create at least one discussion topic.

2.   On the **Team Site,** on the **Team Discussion** page, reply to at least one discussion topic.

3.   On the **Team Site,** use the **People and groups** list to send at least one email to several team members.

4.   Review any emails that you receive from other team members, and reply as necessary.

Lesson 5 Lab 1

Working Remotely with SharePoint Content

Activity Time: 15 minutes

Scenario:

You and some of your team members need to attend a conference in a different location. As you prepare for the meeting that is going to extend for 3 days, you will need to work with your SharePoint team site offline. You need to assign the task of conducting interview to your assistant, Renee Baker when you are away from office. In order to assign the task, you will need to access the SharePoint team site using your mobile.

1. Access a SharePoint list or library offline and edit the library or list.

2. Access the **Tasks** list in the OGC site using the mobile view and assign a ask to **Renee Baker** to conduct interview.

Lesson 6 Lab 1

Customizing the SharePoint Environment

Activity Time: 45 minutes

Scenario:

As an employee of Our Global Company, you will be required to work extensively with the default SharePoint Team Site. Therefore, you will customize a portion of your SharePoint environment effectively.

1. On the **Team Site,** adjust your personal and regional settings to suit your needs.

 Be sure you are working in the **Team Site** and not the **Our Global Company** site.

2. On the **Team Site,** configure at least two alerts on different lists or libraries.

3. On the **Team Site,** subscribe to at least one RSS feed.

4. Initiate some changes to test the alerts and RSS feeds you set up.

5. Personalize your view of the Team Site home page by adjusting the Web Parts.

Lesson 7 Lab 1
Creating a Team Site

Activity Time: 1 hour(s)

Scenario:

As a Senior Consultant at Our Global Company, you have been assigned a new project. Citizens Information Center is expanding to cover regional areas and needs assistance with strategic planning initiatives to ensure the success of the expansion.

1. On the **Our Global Company** site, create a subsite named **CIC##,** where ## is your user number.

 Be sure you are working in the **Our Global Company** subsite and not the **Team Site.**

2. Create a meeting workspace for the CIC## subsite.

3. Add lists and libraries to the CIC## subsite.

4. Create a survey to collect information on the feedback from customers for the CIC## subsite.

5. If necessary, grant access to the CIC## subsite.

Lesson 8 Lab 1
Performing Basic Site Administration

Activity Time: 40 minutes

Scenario:

As the Senior Consultant working on the Citizens Information Center project for Our Global Company, it is your responsibility to manage and maintain the CIC## subsite.

1. Adjust the membership of the Team Owners, Team Members, and Team Visitors groups for CIC##.

 Make sure that you do not change the permissions associated with your user name, or you will not be able to complete this activity.

2. Change the CIC## site's look and feel to reflect your tastes and needs.

3. Customize the **New** drop-down menu for those lists and libraries that have multiple content types.

Solutions

Lesson 1

Activity 1-1

1. **What are the main goals of collaboration technology?**

   Sharing information and enabling communication among team members.

2. **With the rest of the class, brainstorm examples of collaboration technology. Then, discuss the resulting list of examples.**

   Answers might include: Microsoft SharePoint Foundation 2010, email, chat, discussion forums, and blogs. Email helps you to communicate and share files with others in a secured manner. Chat helps you to share information informally and quickly. Discussion forums enable you to discuss issues with multiple users online by posting your query or idea on a website. Blogs enable you to share official or personal information on a special web page that you create and obtain feedback or comments from readers.

3. **Which of these could be considered collaborative technology?**

   a) A Microsoft Excel spreadsheet with OLE links to a Microsoft Access database.

   b) A static web page that describes a company's organization.

   ✓ c) An email program such as Microsoft Outlook.

   ✓ d) A dynamic web page that enables colleagues to share information via discussion boards, blogs, and shared documents.

4. **What are the main components of a Microsoft SharePoint Foundation site?**

   ✓ a) Top-level site

   b) Sidebar

   ✓ c) Subsite

   d) Database

5. **Which of these SharePoint components is created using a default site template and is intended to facilitate team collaboration?**

    a) Subsite

    ✓ b) Team Site

    c) Corporate Website

    d) Top-level site

6. **True or False? The two most common categories of content structures in a SharePoint site are pictures and libraries.**

    ___ True

    ✓ False

Glossary

alert
An email notification that site content has changed.

announcements
A SharePoint list that contains short new items or status updates.

blog
An online journal that can be read and commented on by anyone with access to the site.

calendar
A SharePoint list that tracks team meetings, events, and holidays.

collaboration technology
Software that enables a group of individuals to achieve a common goal by facilitating information sharing and communication.

contacts
A SharePoint list of individuals or groups.

discussion board
A method of communication that allows individuals to read messages, post messages, and reply to messages in an online forum.

issue tracking
A SharePoint list that tracks one or more tasks that are not related to a specific project.

links
A SharePoint list of links from the Internet or your company intranet.

list view
A format for displaying items in a list.

list
A content structure that contains a group of similar items.

message thread
A series of messages posted in relation to a single topic.

Microsoft SharePoint Foundation 2010
A collaboration software from Microsoft.

Microsoft SharePoint Server 2010
A server application that extends the functionality of SharePoint Foundation 2010.

mobile URL
A SharePoint web address ending in /m.

page view
A format for displaying content on a page.

personal view
The customized view of a list, library, or page on a site.

project tasks
A SharePoint list that tracks tasks for a single project.

Really Simple Syndication feed
See RSS feed.

review
A SharePoint list that tracks the software issues related to a type of list.

RSS feed
(Really Simple Syndication feed) XML file formats that are used to deliver the frequently updated content of a website to any application that has feed reader capabilities.

shared view
The default view of a page on a site.

SharePoint library
A content structure that contains files.

site collection
A virtual logical container that contains one or more elements for grouping sites and subsites.

survey
A SharePoint list that records user responses to specific list of questions.

tasks
A SharePoint list of action items for a team or project.

team site
The central location through which team members can access information and communicate with other team members.

top-level site
The first site in a WSS hierarchy.

Tree View
A navigation tool that displays the content of a SharePoint site in a hierarchy.

trigger mail
An email that is sent to authorized users whenever an item is posted on a discussion board.

version
A copy of a document that is created each time the file is modified.

web part
The basic design element of a SharePoint site.

wiki links
Links that use wiki syntax to connect between pages or between sections of a page of a wiki.

wiki
A collection of web pages that contain information created by an online community.

workspace
A SharePoint site that supports team collaboration related to one specific meeting or document.

Index